LANCASTER TARGET

The story of a crew who flew from Wickenby

Jack Currie

LARGE PRINT

Oxford

Copyright © The Estate of Jack Currie, 1977

First published in Great Britain 1981
by Goodall

Published in Large Print 2006 by ISIS Publishing Ltd.,
7 Centremead, Osney Mead, Oxford OX2 0ES
by arrangement with
Crécy Publishing Limited

The moral right of the author has been asserted

British Library Cataloguing in Publication Data
Currie, Jack
Lancaster target : the story of a crew who flew from
Wickenby. – New ed., Large print ed. –
(Isis reminiscence series)
1. Great Britain. Royal Air Force. Bomber Command
2. World War, 1939–1945 – Aerial operations,
British
3. Large type books
I. Title
940.5'44941

ISBN 978–0–7531–9384–6 (hb)
ISBN 978–0–7531–9385–3 (pb)

Printed and bound in Great Britain by
T. J. International Ltd., Padstow, Cornwall

Contents

Preface

In writing this story, I have tried to tell the truth about what happened to the bomber crew of which I was the pilot in 1943 and early 1944. I have been guided by some notes I made at the time, and I have an ill-kept diary, my log-book and some of the navigator's charts. The rest is from my memory, which after more than thirty years may not, I am afraid, be faultless. So, if I have attributed words or deeds to people who did not say or do them, I am sorry. The words, or something very like them, were said, and the deeds were done.

I have tried not to let hindsight alter the views of the scene that I had then. So much has happened in the world since 1943 to change our perspective about bombing — Dresden, Hiroshima, Suez, Vietnam — that it is not easy to remember how the ordinary aircrew of those days looked upon their task. I think we took the view that we were in one hell of a battle for survival, and that we had to do, without too many qualms, the duties for which we were selected and equipped.

It has been said that the whole bomber campaign was so much wasted effort. All warfare is a bitter waste, of men, materials and effort, but I do not like to think that some 50,000 young men of Bomber Command lost their lives for nothing. I am not qualified to argue their case, I have only tried to tell the story of one crew who were lucky enough to survive.

CHAPTER
ONE

First, Pick Your Crew

The sound of the airmen's voices echoed from the high ceilings and misted windows of the drill-hangar. A Wellington hummed overhead in the sparkling morning air. It was the last day of 1942. I stood among the other sergeant-pilots and, trying not to stare at anyone in particular, looked round the assembled groups of aircrew. There were bomb-aimers, navigators, wireless-operators and gunners, and I needed one of each to form my crew. I didn't know any of them; up to now my Air Force world had been peopled by pilots. This was a crowd of strangers. I had a sudden recollection of standing in a suburban dancehall, wondering which girl I should approach. I remembered that it wasn't always the prettiest or the smartest girl who made the best companion for the evening. Anyway, this wasn't the same as choosing a dancing partner, it was more like picking out a sweetheart or a wife, for better or for worse. I needed four of these men to fly with, live with, go to war with. If, as I planned, we went on from Wellingtons to heavy bombers, I would have to find another gunner and an engineer later in our training, but the five of us who came together now would be the nucleus of the crew.

I hadn't realised that the crewing-up procedure would be so haphazard, so unorganised. If I'd known it was going to be like this I'd have given it some previous thought, but I'd imagined that the process would be just as impersonal as most others that we went through in the RAF. I thought I would simply see an order on the notice-board, detailing who was crewed with whom. But what had happened was quite different. When we had all paraded in the hangar, and the roll had been called, the Chief Ground Instructor got up on a dais. He wished us good morning, told us we were there for crewing-up, and said: "Right, chaps, sort yourselves out." Then he jumped off the dais and left us to get on with it.

I decided on an order of priorities to follow, and directed my attention first towards the group of navigators. But how was I to pick one? I couldn't assess what his aptitude with a map and dividers might be from his face, or his skill with a sextant from the size of his feet. I noticed that a wiry little Australian was looking at me anxiously. He took a few steps forward, eyes puckered in a diffident smile, and spoke:

"Looking for a good navigator?"

I walked to meet him. He was an officer. I looked down into his eyes, and received an impression of honesty, intelligence and nervousness. He said:

"You needn't worry, I did all right on the course!"

I held out my hand.

"Jack Currie."

"I'm Jim Cassidy. Have you got a bomb-aimer? I know a real good one — he comes from Brisbane, like me. I'll fetch him over."

The bomb-aimer had a gunner in tow and while we were sizing each other up, we were joined by a tall wireless-operator, who introduced himself in a gentle Northumbrian accent and suggested that it was time for a cup of tea. As we walked to the canteen, I realised that I hadn't made a single conscious choice.

There followed three weeks in Ground School, and a week on leave, before we started to fly the Wellington. Deep in the woodland west of Derby, whenever an aeroplane was serviceable and the February weather permitted, we pounded the Church Broughton circuit and the neighbouring airspace; dual and solo, overshoots and landings, on two engines and on one, with flap and without, cross-country and bombing, air-firing and beam approach. Then we started the whole cycle again by night. I signed a paper which certified that I had received instruction about the fuel and oil systems, and that I thoroughly understood the manipulation of the appropriate controls. We went to the daily flight briefings, studied the met reports, tried to remember where the balloon barrages were, and what to do if we forgot. We practised instrument flying in the Link Trainer, where it didn't matter if we finished the landing fifty feet below the runway, because the little hooded cockpit never left its platform in the ground school. We talked of QDM and ETA, of cloud-base and safety-height, alto-stratus and cumulonimbus, engine heat and Constant Speed Unit, position report and Standard Beam Approach, terminal velocity and infra-red photography, of dewpoint and occlusion.

Snow fell, heavily and quietly, in the night. Next morning, the hangars stood out black and stark in a world of gleaming white. Many of the Australians were seeing snow for the first time, and they greeted it like schoolboys, with boisterous delight. Vigorous skirmishes with snowballs broke out all over the camp, and sporadic sniping still continued when we were all given spades and shovels, and told to get the runway cleared in time for night flying. We worked through the morning and part of the afternoon, but then a freshening wind sprang up, which tugged at the turned-up collars of our greatcoats, numbed our fingers, and made our labours as frustrating as those of Sisyphus. Anyway, we had done enough to make the runway useable if no more snow fell.

That evening, I sat in the flight office with half a dozen other pilots, waiting for the Duty Instructor's call from Flying Control which would tell us whether we would fly or not. The wind now blew in gusts of increasing intensity, and differing views were held about our chances. One pilot said:

"Call this a wind? Listen, when I was training in Canada, we often used to fly in fifty-mile-an-hour blizzards. Thought nothing of it."

Another looked up from a magazine.

4

"Yeah, but in Canada you used to leave the snow on the runway, didn't you? It's all right landing on hard-packed snow."

A third joined in:

"Trouble is, we've got this runway partly cleared. Now it'll have a sprinkling on top that'll freeze over. Be like landing on ice. I reckon it'd be bloody suicidal. And I'm too young, too gay to die. Besides, I've got a date in Derby at eight o'clock."

The telephone bell buzzed. Everyone sprang for the receiver, but I was nearest.

"Yes, sir? I see. Night flying cancelled. What time do you want us in the morning? Thank you, sir. Good-night."

The flight office was empty by the time I had put the phone down.

As we got to know each other better, the strangers in uniform became people, with their individual likes and dislikes, their own attitudes to the war, to discipline, to girls, to food. I found out how often they used the same catch-phrases, were depressed, washed, wrote home, boasted. Cassidy and the bomb-aimer didn't drink, but the gunner, the wireless-operator and I did. We found a small inn at the village on the northern boundary of the airfield. There we were privileged to share with Buzzard Marshall's crew the landlady's favours, which included the use of her kitchen for bacon, eggs and sausages after hours, and the company of her daughters. The eldest of these was a big, untidy, cuddlesome girl whose efforts to keep her relations with us on a sisterly basis weren't always successful.

For the last half-hour or so before closing time, the epicure Marshall sipping gin and vermouth, and the rest of us downing the clear, bitter ale they brew beside the Trent, we liked to sing at the piano, while the village postmistress pounded an accompaniment. Her repertoire was limited to hymn tunes and a few songs of the day, of which we favoured "Roll out the Barrel", "Bless 'em All" and, for the Australians' sake, "Waltzing Matilda". To the embarrassment of Charles Fairbairn, the wireless-operator, there would be girlish appeals for him to play his tuba. These requests, which would be loudly reinforced by the rest of us, resulted from a foolery of mine. It had seemed to me that the Australians, with their sun-tanned faces their royal-blue uniform, and those distinctive accents which made you think of a mid-western cowboy influenced by the sound of Bow Bells, had a head start on the reticent Fairbairn when it came to girl-appeal. Thinking to add a little colour to his personality, I had let it be known, in his absence, that in civil life he had been one of the nation's leading tuba-players. It was a perversity to establish a reputation for him in the field of music, as he couldn't whistle the national anthem in tune, but it was a memory of Gary Cooper playing the tuba in a movie that had prompted me, for Fairbairn had something of the actor's slow, quiet style. I had also told the girls that, despite his fame, Fairbairn was inordinately modest. So his anguished disclaimers of any virtuosity were brushed aside, and they besought

6

him all the more to entertain them. Marshall joined the plot.

"It's his fingering that's so good, you see. That's what makes him such a wizard on the old Morse buzzer."

Fairbairn shook his head, and smiled wearily. At last he gained relief by admitting that he had left the instrument in the cloakroom at Derby station, and mislaid the ticket.

Crews usually kept their own company, but it was considered all right for the pilot of one crew to associate with the pilot of another on occasion, or indeed one navigator with another, and so on. But for, say, a gunner to be in company with the pilot of another crew more than once or twice would be thought unnatural and disloyal. Girls were another matter, and in that case it was every man for himself. I had little time and less money to spend on girls, but there did seem to be a lot of them about, and it had to be admitted that they were very agreeable.

The Friary Hotel in Derby was another haven, with an urban opulence far removed from the comradely comforts of the village inn beside the airfield. Supreme authority at the Friary rested in the dread, seldom-seen person of Miss Whittaker, who ruled from a shadowy office in the heart of the old-fashioned building. Seated at a massive desk, she glared with unblinking severity over gold-rimmed half-glasses, and issued her edicts in a ringing baritone voice. But I found that the dragon would forgive misdemeanours, waive unpaid accounts, even proffer small loans, without the slightest change in her forbidding expression. The sardonic head waiter also revealed himself a friend to the impecunious pilot, contriving to serve two dinners for the price of one, when I was bold enough to entertain one of the glittering girls from the glamorous clientele of the cocktail bar.

One or another of these charming creatures was occasionally claimed by the prosperous patron to whom she owed her luxurious life-style, and would be absent for a while. Then she would reappear, yet better bedecked and sleeker than before, to dispense her favours at leisure. Not for these ladies the encumbering infants who littered the lives of the airfield inn girls, not in their primrose paths would I find the blunt, battle-dressed men of the bomber crews. Here was the sound and the scent of a different social scene, which for me complemented the other, more homely, *menage*. Here, too, I met an amusing companion in Steve, a curly-haired, cheerful fighter pilot with a fund of good stories. Perhaps the best, and certainly the longest of these concerned one Pilot Officer Fotheringay-Jones. It seems that this paragon arrived on posting to a Spitfire squadron, and reported to the Flight Commander, a Squadron Leader Watson, who said:

"Fotheringay-Jones, eh? Jolly good show! Glad to have you with us. Now, the first thing you'll want to do is to gen up on station standing orders, station routine orders, the flight order book, pilot's notes and so on."

"Actually, sir, no. I want to get in the air."

"Eh?"

"In the air, sir. I want to fly a Spitfire."

"Yes, yes, Fotheringay-Jones, of course, all in good time . . ."

"No, sir, now. I see one is ready at the hangar for air test; may I take it up?"

"Oh, very well, Fotheringay-Jones. I don't want to quench your commendable zeal. You can attend to the admin this afternoon."

Within minutes Fotheringay-Jones was airborne. Not only airborne, but beating up the squadron offices at very low level. As the Spitfire flashed by his window for the third time, Watson attempted to have Fotheringay-Jones recalled by Flying Control, only to find that the pilot had omitted to turn on his RT. Meanwhile, the Station Commander, Group Captain Ponsonby, was dealing with some correspondence in his headquarters, which now attracted Fotheringay-Jones's attention. As the Spitfire made his windows rattle, flashing past inverted at nought feet, the Station Commander ducked instinctively. He then picked up the telephone and directed a tirade at the unfortunate Watson for permitting such dangerous antics, and demanded an explanation.

Fotheringay-Jones eventually tired of his attempts to terrorise the station and flight commanders, and landed off a stall-turn in the circuit, flicking his wheels down at the last possible minute. As he climbed out of the cockpit, he was met by an agitated mechanic with a message from Squadron Leader Watson to report to him immediately, if not sooner.

When Fotheringay-Jones sauntered in, Watson looked at him coldly:

"I suppose you think you're very clever. You have the mistaken impression that you are an ace. Well, Fotheringay-Jones, let me tell you that you are not. You are a dangerous young fool. Had you taken the trouble to read the flight order book, as I suggested, you would have known that low flying is most strictly prohibited. As for your extraordinary behaviour in dive-bombing the admin buildings, your failure to observe RT discipline, your irregular manoeuvres in the aerodrome circuit, I shall say no more for the moment. I am bound to tell you that you have managed to incur not only my serious displeasure, but also that of the Station Commander, all within a few moments of arriving on this squadron."

Fotheringay-Jones eyed him calmly.

"Have you quite finished, sir?"

"For the moment, yes."

"Then you can go and get stuffed."

"I beg your pardon?"

"Go and get stuffed."

Watson was appalled. Dismissing Fotheringay-Jones from his presence, he reported the outcome of his interview to the Station Commander, concluding:

"I'm afraid he was rather insolent, sir."

"What did he say?"

"I would prefer not to repeat it, sir."

"Out with it, man!"

"Well, sir, he told me to get stuffed."

"Did he, indeed? I can see that I shall have to deal with this fellow myself. What did you say his name was?"

"Fotheringay-Jones, sir."

"Bring him to my office, Watson. Immediately."

When Fotheringay-Jones had been run to earth in the bar of the officers' mess, the further interview took place, and Group Captain Ponsonby administered a similar rocket to that delivered by Squadron Leader Watson, but on a far grander scale. When he had thundered to his climax, Fotheringay-Jones, who had been shuffling his feet for some time, looked up and spoke:

"Go and have a good shit."

After a moment's horrified silence Watson, by now appalled almost to bursting point, motioned the pilot out and awaited the great man's wrath. Spluttering horribly, the Station Commander sent for Fotheringay-Jones's documents. The adjutant laid them in front of his master, who instructed Watson to read them aloud:

"Elementary Flying School — 'A highly proficient student'. Basic Flying School — 'Well above the average'. Advanced Flying School — 'Exceptional'. Operational Conversion Unit — 'An exceptional student who will make an outstanding operational pilot'. Further remarks — 'Pilot Officer Fotheringay-Jones is a nephew of HM Secretary of State for Air'."

Group Captain Ponsonby knocked out his pipe in the ash-tray on his desk, and stood up purposefully:

"That will be all, Watson. For myself, I am just going to the lavatory. You, I have no doubt, will make your own arrangements."

★ ★ ★

We were approaching the end of our Wellington training when Cassidy's appendix began to give him trouble. He was taken into Derby Hospital for treatment, and we learned that at least a fortnight would elapse before he could rejoin the crew. He expressed a fear that he might lose his place:

"You won't go on to HCU without me, Jack, will you? I had a chat with the Nav Leader, and he said he'd talk to the Flight Commander. If you'll be in it, they'll screen you for a few trips until I'm fit."

The request was reasonable enough, both personally and officially; I didn't want to lose Jimmy, and it would be uneconomical to disrupt a pilot-navigator team which had established a good working relationship for the sake of a couple of weeks' inaction. So I flew in the Wellington's right-hand seat with new boys on cross-country flights, and awaited Cassidy's return. Charlie Fairbairn, the lanky wireless-operator, wisely found some similar employment in his own field, but I wasn't so lucky with the other members of the crew. The fair-haired handsome gunner flew as spare with another crew, which crashed with total loss of life. The darkly earnest bomb-aimer was transferred to a different course and, within weeks of leaving us, had joined the long list of those missing, believed killed, in action. When Cassidy returned from Derby, pale but eager, only the skeleton of a crew remained: the navigator, the wireless-operator and me. But not for long. We gained reinforcements (if that be the word) from the awkward squad. The first was a stocky bomb-aimer from Melbourne, who had been held over from a previous course; the second was a West Australian gunner, who introduced himself to me in the sergeants' mess lavatory one morning after breakfast. Standing in the stall beside me, he fixed me with a cold, blue gaze:

"You Currie?"

"Yes."

"I'm Lanham. I'm your new rear-gunner."

"Oh, good. How d'you do?"

"I'm fine. Do you drink?"

"Beg your pardon?"

The Australian, dapper in his well-pressed battledress, buttoned his trousers and frowned impatiently.

"Do you drink alcohol?"

"Sometimes. Why?"

"I don't reckon grog goes with flying. My last pilot drank too much — that's why I clocked him one."

I looked at the gunner with a new interest. He was about five foot six, muscular, twenty-six or twenty-seven years old.

"You had a scrap with your pilot?"

"He reported it, the whinging blighter. Trouble was, I was a flight sarnt and he was a flight looey, so I got the chop. I lost my crown, and did six months in the Orkneys as Aerodrome Control Pilot."

"I see."

Stuck out by the runway caravan with a Very pistol; it was a lonely, cold and boring job in the Midlands. In the Orkneys it must have been a salutary punishment indeed. Lanham continued to regard me sternly.

"I don't reckon grog mixes with flying, and I aim to survive this war."

"So do I. And just to set your mind at rest, I only drink on leave or stand-downs."

"You want to cut that out too, skipper. Grog slows your reactions."

As I walked to the flight office, I couldn't help thinking about the loss of two good crewmen and their replacement by a bomb-aimer of dubious potential and a recalcitrant rear-gunner with a bee in his bonnet.

As time passed, however, I began to savour the personalities of the newcomers, and even to enjoy their contributions to the corporate style of the crew. Larry Myring, the bomb-aimer, was a happy grumbler who alternately groaned and giggled his heavy way through the real or imagined rights and wrongs of life. He maintained a nebulous liaison with a woman, whom he variously referred to as "the missus", "that bloody whore" (in moments of affection) and sometimes by the name of Freda. This lady, curiously painted and certainly pregnant, would appear in bars and cafes where we refreshed ourselves, and station herself at a distance until Larry's flickering eye noticed her presence. Muttering curses, he would excuse himself and join her in quiet but animated conversation. All too often the exchanges would become obviously acrimonious, and were only ended by the grudging passage of coin from him to her.

I gained a clue to Larry's winning way with a woman when Freda came to witness our Wellington's return from a practice bombing sortie. She stood close beyond the wired perimeter fencing, unwittingly behind the aircraft's engines, and awaited her man's descent from the front turret. With moustache twitching and eyes quite squinting in anticipation, he thrust his face into mine:

"Do us a favour, skip, and give 'er the gun before you shut the engines down. Blow the bitch's skirts up!"

Cruelly complying, I opened the throttles fully against the brakes. Larry squealed with satisfaction as the airflow not only disarrayed the lady's dress, but deposited her on the muddy footpath, bottom first.

Charlie Lanham smiled coolly at this prank, but it needed no words to tell what opinion of Myring he had formed; he found the bomb-aimer uncouth and obtuse. His own brand of fun was light and happy, harming nobody. His ways proclaimed a sense of rhythm and of balance. He played the banjo and the mouth organ, sang and whistled like a flock of birds. He walked on his hands, rode a bicycle while standing in the saddle, and had muscles like a mini-Samson. From the moment of our meeting until our tour was nearly over, it seemed that Lanham was chirruping beside me, swaggering a little with his athlete's step, and cajoling me to be the sort of captain that he wanted.

Pilfering had been practically unknown in the United States, where I had learned to fly. Here it was more common, and I lost several belongings before I got into the habit of taking greater care of them. I was really appalled when my service cap was removed from the entrance hall in the sergeants' mess. It had taken nearly two years to crumple it into that comfortably ravaged condition. It was faded to a dirty neutral colour, like the sea under a winter overcast, and it fitted my head as snugly as if it had been moulded on. Why should anyone who wanted to steal a cap choose mine, which must have been the most disreputable on view? I scoured the camp for it, wearing a discarded cap of Fairbairn's, but it had gone for ever. I had to draw a new one from the stores, and recommence the long process of wearing-in.

Next to go were the front and rear lamps from my bicycle. Their loss didn't distress me like that of the cap had done, but it caused more trouble. I couldn't afford to buy new ones, and I wasn't going to sink to stealing other people's. On the other hand, I certainly wasn't going to stay in camp while the rest of the crew were out on the spree. So I was riding between Myring and Fairbairn, who both had lamps, when we returned one night from a trip to a pub at Hatton. We were a couple of miles from the camp, singing happily and keeping pretty good formation, full of beer and *bonhomie*, when we saw another cyclist coming towards us. This turned out to be the local bobby, and he called on me to stop. He spoke slowly and majestically:

"Are you aware that you are not displaying a white front light as required by the Road Transport Lighting Act of 1927?"

"Yes, I know. It was pinched, I'm afraid."

The policeman dismounted, propped his own bicycle carefully against the kerb, and examined mine closely.

"Hm . . . Are you further aware that you are not displaying a red rear light as required by the Lighting Restriction Order of 1940?"

"Yes, it was pinched, too. That's why I'm riding in convoy with these chaps."

He took a notebook from his breast pocket.

"You understand I shall have to report this, Sergeant?"

"Oh, come on, Constable. It's twelve o'clock at night. there's not a soul on the road . . ."

"I was, wasn't I?"

He had me there. I was beginning to realise that we weren't going to get along. He poised a pencil over his notebook, and looked at me enquiringly.

"What might your name be?"

I was about to say that it might be Julius Caesar when Larry decided to take a hand. Staggering slightly, he approached the constable and, emitting a visible cloud of beer fumes, addressed him in what was presumably meant to be an ingratiating manner:

"Ah, don't be a bloody drongo, sport! We've 'ad a coupla grogs, and now we're going back to camp to get on with the war."

Larry now found it necessary to retain his balance by leaning heavily on the constable's shoulder. He continued:

"So jus' stick yer notebook back in yer pocket, and forget all about it, eh, cobber?"

I couldn't tell whether Fairbairn was chuckling or getting hiccups, but Larry was clearly getting nowhere with the grim officer of the law, who stepped firmly out of his embrace and readdressed himself to me:

"I hope I shan't have to ask you to accompany me to the station."

I passed him my identity card.

"There you are, you miserable sod, and I hope you're pleased with your night's work. You ought to be on Hitler's side — you'd do bloody well in the Gestapo. And I hope your rabbits die."

I was fined five shillings a couple of weeks later at Stratton Court House. Larry Myring represented me, because I was on an air-firing exercise. The magistrate said he would have taken a more lenient view of the offence if it hadn't been for the abusive language I'd offered to the constable. Larry had giggled when it was all read out in court, and he'd been soundly ticked off by the magistrate.

Lanham didn't insist on total abstinence during the comparative inaction that followed Cassidy's illness, so I took the Derby road occasionally to join the playful company at the Friary's cocktail bar. One of the regular clientele was an engineer called Douglas Seaford, who had previously introduced himself by the simple expedient of buying me a drink. He was a tall, insouciant fellow, a few years older than I, who had served his apprenticeship with Rolls-Royce, and now worked with another Derby firm making aircraft components. He had an engaging manner, a comfortable apartment and, by my standards, a considerable supply of money. He also had an eccentric sense of

18

humour, for the exercise of which he seemed to need the encouragement of a similarly irresponsible companion.

A number of stag's heads were mounted in the hotel's ill-lit corridors. These trophies, together with the grim grandfather clocks, brass gongs, Victorian tapestries and massive, gilt-framed landscape paintings, helped to imbue the place with its uniquely spooky atmosphere. Seaford believed that the great beasts' heads, so noble and aloof in their expression, were improved by the addition of lighted cigarettes dangling from the corners of their mouths. I had to admit that it gave them a rakish, worldly look which was faintly amusing. Another impulse persuaded us that it would be diverting if he were to wear his suit, and I my uniform, back to front, and then walk backwards into the cocktail bar. Seaford also liked to eat the floral decorations, and to rearrange the shoes that residents left outside their bedrooms to be cleaned.

In due course Seaford met the rest of the crew, and got on well with them. He had the nice habit of doing little services for his acquaintances, and there was always a spare bed at his flat for any of us who missed the last bus back to camp. It was pretty clear that he relished the company of flying men, but that he felt some unease about not being in uniform himself. If he could have escaped from his reserved occupation, I think his wish would have been to fly with us. Maybe it was subconscious recognition of these feelings that moved me to an escapade which would have got me into awful trouble if it had been discovered.

Lanham and I had spent a couple of days in London, and when we returned to Derby from King's Cross, Seaford met us at the station and treated us to lunch. After the meal, when Seaford was laughing at Lanham's views of London life, I broached my idea:

"Listen, Doug. How would you like a trip in the Wimpey?"

He held a coffee-cup suspended between the saucer and his mouth, and his eyes grew as round as the saucer. He said:

"Mm. I'd like it."

"Can you get the afternoon off?"

"This afternoon? Are you serious?"

We've got an air test at three o'clock. We'll take you on it."

Seaford rubbed his hands together, and a smile spread across his face, but Lanham looked at me doubtfully.

"How're you going to swing it, Jack? It's not exactly in the book."

"Piece of cake. We smuggle him into our hut the back way, and kit him out in Fairbairn's battledress. They're about the same size, and Fairbairn can wear his best blue."

Lanham chuckled.

"Yeah, he'll love that. Wearing his best blue in a nasty, dirty Wellington. He keeps it in moth balls and tissue-paper."

I ignored the comment.

"You draw an extra chute and Mae West for Doug, then we just take him with us on the transport to the kite. Who's ever going to know?"

Seaford tried to get the grin off his face. He said:

"Jack, I'm not going to have you getting into trouble on my account . . ."

"Are you trying to back out of it?"

"No, but . . ."

"Right, then. Just don't blab it around. If it got back to any of the staff that I'd taken a civvy flying, I'd be for the high jump."

In the event, it went without a hitch. We not only flew a forty-five-minute night flying test in Wellington 975G with a supernumerary crewman, who wore an ill-fitting battledress and a big grin, but took him to supper in the sergeants' mess, and quartered him in our billet for the night.

Later that week, with Cassidy back at work in the navigation compartment, we resumed our training programme at the point where it was interrupted. A high-level bombing exercise and a cross-country flight, both by night, would complete the course for us, and these we carried out in early May. Then we were briefed for a leaflet raid on occupied French territory, a mission which was code-named Nickel, and which was meant to let us have a taste, however mild, of action. However, the flight was cancelled for some reason not divulged to us, and the piles of paper propaganda were returned to store. We were clear at last to go on to the last stage of our training.

The Flight Commander stuck a form in my log-book and wrote on it: "Above the average". He told me I was going on Lancasters, and I felt a tingle of pleasure. Bomber Command had two other types of heavies — the Stirling and the Halifax but I knew that the Avro Lancaster was the best of all bombers. As we hurried around the camp with our clearance chits, the news came through of 617 Squadron's raid on the West German dams. They had breached two, and damaged a third, with their special bombs that bounced on water. Considering the difficulties of low-level navigation at night, and the hazards of the bombing-run, we thought they had done well to get eleven Lancasters back to Scampton out of the nineteen that had set out.

We travelled to the Heavy Conversion Unit at Lindholme, north of Doncaster, looking forward to a brief stay at a comfortable pre-war station for the last phase of our training. But the spacious brick-built quarters were not for us. With the other crews from OTU we were segregated like a leper colony, in a muddy little hutted camp a couple of miles away from the airfield. For four depressing days, we ran about in our white vests and baggy blue shorts, doing PT and other violent exercises. By the end of the second day Lanham and I had had a bellyful of the prison-camp atmosphere, so we metaphorically crawled under the wire and hitch-hiked into Doncaster in search of a meal and a change of scene. The few shillings we had between us might have bought a snack at the YMCA, but we wanted better than that. So it looked as though Lanham's Ronson cigarette-lighter would have to go, if we could find a market for it. Despite the troubles with the bobby at Church Broughton, I still had faith in the police force, and I asked a patrolling constable whether there happened to be a pawnshop in Doncaster. He loomed over me, and balanced himself delicately on the balls of his feet.

"I don't think you'll find a pawnshop open at this time of the evening, sir."

Lanham pushed his cap back, and groaned.

"We've been shaking every tree along the road from Lindholme, but never a penny fell out. I reckon we'll have to find some joker who'll buy this lighter."

"Bit short of ready cash?"

"Are we ever? And we're starving. They don't feed us at camp. It's really cruel. Oh, the officers do all right, even the airmen, but there's no food for NCOs."

The constable smiled, and pointed a large hand down the High Street.

"Go down to the Guildhall, and ask for Sergeant Hather. He might be able to help you."

We found the good sergeant in his office, and explained our plight. He took a pound note out of his pocket, and handed it to Lanham. Then he unlocked a drawer in his desk, dropped the lighter inside it, and said:

"It'll be here whenever you come back for it, lads."

We dined at the Danum Hotel, and drank to the health and success of the Doncaster Constabulary.

Having exhausted us with PT and malnutrition, the powers that be at Lindholme sent us to their satellite airfield Blyton, near the town of Gainsborough. There the crew was augmented by a flight engineer and another gunner, which brought us up to the heavy-bomber complement of seven. Both the newcomers were sergeants, and younger than the rest of us. Indeed, George Protheroe, the little Welshman who was to fly in the mid-upper turret looked, with his bright eyes and cherubic cheeks, even younger than his seventeen years. The flight engineer's name was Walker and therefore, willy-nilly, Johnny. He came from the pleasant little hills of Cheshire, stood tall and slim and was blessed with fair good looks. Walker and I were airborne in the Halifax together on our first day at Blyton, under the supervision of an instructor in the morning, and solo in the afternoon. We dropped the gunners off at Binbrook, where they spent the next week with a gunnery training unit, getting to know each other and working out their tactics. Meanwhile, Walker and I did a lot of feathering drills and three-engined flying, Myring practised map-reading and Fairbairn worked the W/T stations for bearings. We made a detour to Church Broughton village, where I flew low above the inn, banking steeply to pick out the chickens scampering in the garden, then circling back to see the women running out to wave at us, as they realised that the engine noise was not that of the local Wellingtons.

In addition to the greater power of its Rolls-Royce Merlins, the Halifax V was bigger, heavier, less manoeuvrable, and had more gadgets and more instruments than any aeroplane I'd flown before. But it was stable in flight, spacious, had good visibility, and on landing sat down on three points with a satisfying thud.

I guessed that we used it for four-engine conversion to save the more potent Lancaster from damage at our unpractised hands.

Douglas Seaford, our aerophile friend from Derby, came to see us, beaming with delight because he'd just got permission to join the RAF as a technical officer. By way of celebration, we let him buy us a few drinks at a gloomy pub in Gainsborough, then slipped him, with the ease of practise, into Fairbairn's battledress to spend the night in our Nissen hut at Blyton. Next morning Seaford went on his way, rejoicing, and we completed our training on the Halifax. The Lancasters of the Finishing School were now at our disposal. For a week I had been looking at them as they stood in their dispersals, longing to be through with the Halifax, and to climb into one of those tall cockpits. Much of what we were told in Ground School about the Lancaster made little impression on me; my notebooks were filled with diagrams, graphs and formulae, but what I really learned was from my senses, from the sight, feel, smell and sound of the aircraft.

The Lancaster looked good from every angle, strongly shaped and well proportioned. In flight she appeared both powerful and balanced. Some aeroplanes seem to lean forward anxiously as they fly, others to be protestingly pushed along from behind, but the Lancaster rode the air easily and steadily. It's the same in sport, when a great batsman walks out to the wicket, or the world's best heavyweight steps into the ring, you get a thrill of recognition. Champions have an aura of their own.

You boarded the Lancaster either through a door at the rear of the fuselage, starboard side, or by climbing a ladder into the nose. The cockpit smelled good, and the pilot's seat was comfortable, with a good view from port quarter to starboard beam. All the crew were pleased with their stations, and none more than the bomb-aimer, who had a panoramic view through his perspex blister in the nose. He lay on the padded door of the nose hatch to operate the bombsight, and, if he had to man the front gun turret, all he had to do was to stand up and grab the triggers. Back over the hatch and up a step you came to the cabin, where the pilot and the flight engineer sat side by side up front. If you wanted to get from the nose into the cabin, you would have to get the flight engineer to push his footrest out of the way, and swing his feet up. Then you could crawl under his seat. The navigator sat facing to port, in a little curtained office behind the pilot, and you would have to squeeze past him to reach the wireless-operator's compartment. His was the cosiest place in the aircraft, right next to the hot-air outlet. He also had the astrodome above him, for the navigator's star shots, and the wireless-op could keep a lookout there when he wasn't working the set. Still going aft, you would climb over the wide mass of the main spar, keeping your head down to avoid the escape hatch above it, and then past the rest-bed on your right into the long, dark fuselage. Since you left the nose, you had actually been walking on the roof of the bomb-bay, but now you came to the end of that. You stepped down on to the fuselage floor, and for the first time you could stand upright, at least until you reached the mid-upper turret, shaped like an egg, with the wide end sticking out of the roof. You wriggled past the turret and felt your way on, between the ammunition runways, past the main door and the Elsan lavatory, to reach the rear-turret entrance.

There was a list of things to check before you could start the engines, another list before you moved out of dispersal, and another before take-off. The last were the really important ones, and we called them VAs, for vital actions. These differed slightly from one aeroplane to another, but I liked to stick to the same formula, with modifications according to each aircraft's requirements. So I ran through the sequence TMPFFGGH, which stood for trim, refixture, pitch, fuel, flap, gills, gyro, hydraulics, on the Lancaster, but changed the M to medium gear on the supercharger, because the mixture control was automatic. The flight engineer made some of the checks himself; for example, under F he checked the fuel gauges, checked that the master cocks and booster pumps were turned on, the crossfeed turned off, and selected the right tars and followed me through on the rest.

But the VAs were made at the marshalling point, just before moving on to the runway for take-off. You had to get there from dispersal first, and this was the time when the Lancaster wasn't quite at her best. Having signalled to the ground crew to pull the chocks away from the main wheels, you released the brakes and gave her a firm burst of power on all four engines to get her moving. Then you had to negotiate a narrow, winding perimeter track, which might be more than a mile long if you were starting from the upwind side of the airfield, to reach the take-off point. You turned by gunning the outer engine on the side away from your turn, and straightened up by giving the opposite engine a burst, but there was a lot of inertia, and you had to anticipate each turn by ten or twenty degrees, depending on your speed. You were supposed to taxi at a fast walking-pace, but that wasn't easy to judge, sitting twenty feet above the ground. It was best to keep a ready grip on the brake lever, in case she tried to run away with you.

The first time I flew the Lancaster was on 18 June 1943. A screened pilot sat beside me for the first few take-offs and landings, with Walker standing vigilant behind him. I settled myself snugly in the seat, and felt the rudder pedals with the balls of my feet. I held the rim of the control wheel in my left hand, and opened the throttles with my right, leading with the thumb on the port outer lever to counter the tendency to swing left. I released the brakes, and Lancaster ED414 lurched forward. I kept my eyes on the white-painted centre line of the runway, and continued to push the throttle levers up the quadrant until the port outer lever met the gate that marked full take-off power. As I brought the other three levers up to the gate, I kept a forward pressure on the control wheel to lift the tail off the ground. With the rudders up in the slipstream, it was easy to keep her straight, and I brought the control wheel back gently as she gathered speed. There was plenty of runway still ahead when I felt her wanting to get airborne and gave more strength to the backward pressure on the wheel. She let go of the ground immediately, and two years of training were over: I was a Lancaster pilot.

As the undercarriage folded up and tucked itself into its housing, I brought the engines back to climbing power and gently swung the control wheel left. The horizon tilted, and I looked down the length of the port wing at the airfield below. I saw the tiny, uniformed figures, the bicycles and trucks moving on the roadways of the camp, and rejoiced in the strength of the aircraft climbing in the sunshine at my command.

CHAPTER
TWO

Wickenby

The famous squadron numbers, with their associated crests and mottoes, had been honoured since the distant days of the Royal Flying Corps in World War I. To regular airmen and students of military aviation they conjured up the romance of those early years, and of later actions over Indian hills or Arab coasts; but they meant nothing to the average Australian, New Zealander or Canadian, and little more to us indigenous civilians in uniform. The fighter pilots were more likely to retain their local loyalties, with their city squadrons and their Auxiliary Air Force connections, but we had none of that. It was a matter of pure chance which squadron topped the list for replacements when our turn came for posting. It might be 460 Squadron at Binbrook, 12 at Wickenby, 101 at Ludford Magna, 103 at Elsham Wolds or 100 at Grimsby — what did it matter?

We heard a lot of stories about casualties on the squadrons, how this or that crew we were trained with had "got the chop". Some squadrons were supposed to have better luck than others, better leadership or better maintenance. I felt confident of the Lancaster and of my crew, and paid little attention to the ominous stories.

In the event, we were posted to 12 Squadron at Wickenby. We inferred from the number that it must be one of the oldest squadrons in the service, and Cassidy dug up further information in the Intelligence Library: the badge was a fox's head, the motto was "Leads the Field", and the squadron had won the first two Victoria Crosses of the war. News of more immediate interest was that we had a 36-hour pass before we had to report to the Squadron Commander, Wing Commander Wood, at Wickenby. That wasn't long enough for the journey to Harrow to see my parents, even if I could have raised the train fare, nor did I want to fritter this particular pass away on some local frivolity. Sheffield and its nearby moors lay only thirteen miles from Gainsborough; I had a sudden urge to see again those places of my early memories. I told the crew I was going to visit my Aunt Mabel. Lanham chortled derisively:

"Yeah? I'll bet you are. D'you reckon she'll have a friend for me?"

"On the level, Charlie. And she must be nearly sixty."

"Oh, well. I'm coming with you, anyway."

The journey was more involved than I had realised, and took four hours of our precious thirty-six. It was 9.30p.m. before we arrived, unheralded, at my aunt's lodgings, but she greeted us with Yorkshire hospitality, fed us, moved in with another lodger so that we might have her bedroom, and gave us breakfast in the morning. But there was a price to pay: Auntie worked at the Sheffield Food Office, and there she made us run the gauntlet of her countless female colleagues, all of whom had been indoctrinated with Auntie's fond opinion of my character and talents. That done, we were led into the Food Officer's inner sanctum for formal presentation to the boss. He, it seemed, had also been briefed by Auntie. Ever since wartime shortages began, she had held the view that, as the Roman legionaries needed their salt ration, so did I need a constant supply of razor-blades and cigarettes. Even in America, where the term "in short supply" was never known, her regular parcels of these items reached me. So it was no great surprise when the Food Officer genially heaped packets of Wardonia blades and Player's cigarettes upon us. I was glad that Lanham was there, because with his natural *bonhomie* he reacted more easily to the kindness of these Sheffielders than I, who was born one of them.

Auntie was given the rest of the day off, as of right, and after lunch the three of us set off to gratify my whim. We found the remembered terraced house in Brincliffe Edge, with the grim backyard where I had earned my mother's scoldings for copying the habits and accents of the neighbour boys ("Speak properly not 'Ah'm coomin oop nah, moom'", and "Nice boys go to the lavatory when they want to wee-wee"), and then we took the bus across the moors to Grindleford. There was the blacksmith's shop, and our old Rose Cottage, and The Maynard Arms Hotel, where the Australian cricketers used to come from playing at Bramall Lane. We walked for miles while the great moors loomed about us, Big Moor, White Edge and Eyam, had tea at the Sir William Inn, and regained Grindleford with just sufficient time to cross the footbridge over Burbage Brook, trickling down from Hallam Moor on its way to join the Derwent. My initials, carved into the handrail, were still discernible. Then we hurried to the station, and caught the train which burrowed under Totley Moor, filling the long tunnel with its acrid fumes, puffed and clattered through Dore and Beauchief and brought us back into the smoking bowl of Sheffield. There, in the echoing vaults of the railway station, we said our goodbyes, and Lanham and I went on our way laden with gifts and auntly benedictions.

Wickenby airfield lay ten miles north-east of Lincoln on the near side of the road that winds from Wragby into Market Rasen. We arrived there, via the LNER and the tiny railway halt at Snelland, on Sunday 27 June. Jimmy the navigator disappeared into his officers' quarters, and the rest of us were allocated a wooden hut about half a mile from the sergeants' mess. Our first meeting with a serving member of 12 Squadron occurred in the ablutions building and it was not a happy one. Emerging from a lavatory stall, he looked us over coldly.

"Sprog crew, eh? Just arrived?"

"Yes."

"F . . . your luck. I give you two weeks."

"What are you talking about?"

He leaned against a pillar. Crew-cut hair, pale lined face, broad shoulders, gunner's badge, flight sergeant's tapes and crown on the battledress sleeves. His eyes blinked rapidly.

"We've lost eight kites in the last three ops. New crews hardly get time to unpack. You haven't got a bloody hope with their new night-fighters. And if they don't get you, the predicted flak . . ."

Charlie Lanham interrupted him. Strutting forward like a fighting cock, he thrust his chin up into the speaker's face.

"Shut up, you bloody leper. You're yellow. Piss off and take your whinging mouth with you."

"Okay, okay, digger. Keep your hair on."

He puffed a cigarette from the pocket under his brevet, and walked quickly out.

"Don't pay any attention to him, Jack. He's LMF. I've seen them before."

"Poor bastard."

Later, as we emptied the contents of our kit-bags in the sparsely furnished hut, the little Welsh mid-upper gunner paused in his shrill whistling to ask Lanham:

"What's LMF mean, Charlie?"

"Lack of moral fibre, sport. It means you've got no guts."

"What happens if you're LMF then?"

Lanham was testing the strength of the bedsprings by performing a trampoline act on them. He stopped bouncing to answer Protheroe.

"There are only two ways you can get off aircrew: one's the chop, and the other's LMF. If you go LMF, they get you away from the Squadron as quick as they can, so it doesn't rub off on the other guys. And then they send you to a nice rehabilitation centre, where you can figure out how to explain to the folks back home why you ain't flying no more, and how you came to lose your stripes and brevet. There's a centre like that at Sheffield, and I've heard it's no rest cure, boy."

Protheroe nodded and resumed whistling.

The airfield had been fashioned out of farmland, and named after the hamlet nearby, which name itself — "farm of the Viking" — remembered its long history. Such a farm infringed the northern boundary of the airfield, sheltered by a screen of poplars and fortified by barns and cowsheds, and seemed besieged by crouching bombers. Old rights-of-way, suspended in the grip of war, made fading patterns on the land. The major runway, one mile long, lay across the southern centre of the airfield, running east to west, whence came the average wind. For less usual conditions, when the wind blew otherwise, two subsidiary runways made an X shape on the airfield, seen from the air like a brand mark on the cattle's side.

Against the eastern margin of the field, flight huts and crew rooms hid in a shallow grove of oak, ash, birch and elm trees. Outside the self-protecting huddle of the grove, the winds which swept the level land tore at the emaciated branchlets of solitary trees which marked the ancient lanes and hedgerows.

We walked to the airfield, where the ebbing glow of sunlight was reflected westward by the perspex on Lancaster cabins and turrets and by the wide windows of the watchtower standing square and solid on the edge of the perimeter track. The angry sound of a Merlin engine running roughly came from the other side of the airfield. I sat on the grass and absorbed the scene: a petrol bowser humming towards dispersal, a tractor pulling a long train of bomb trolleys, a faded windsock flapping gently on its mast, and the crimson signature of the sun on a few high lines of cirrus cloud.

Larry, standing beside me, looked at his watch.

"The crews'll have finished their flying meal; we'd better get down to the mess and see if there's any grub left."

The aircrews were emerging from the sergeants' mess as we reached it. We recognised a few faces, and exchanged greetings before entering the littered dining hall. On the counter, a slate bore the chalk-written menu "egg sausages chips". But as we approached, the eggs were deleted by a WAAF waitress. They were for the departing aircrews only. My thoughts were with them as we ate our meal, and as soon as I had finished I returned to my perch on the airfield boundary. Behind the watchtower, among the drab stone and iron buildings, a crew bus was leaving the locker-room. It turned on to the perimeter track and drove off towards the dispersal pans on my left. Another crew bus was filling up, a group of men wearing life-jackets and parachute harnesses passed ration boxes, navigation bags, flying-jackets and parachutes to those inside. The small figure of a red-haired WAAF driver stood by the double doors, helping the encumbered crews aboard.

A motor-bicycle appeared among the trees, threaded a way through the crowd outside the locker-room, and accelerated across the perimeter track. Gravel scraped as the rider braked under the watchtower windows, and the motor stammered and stopped as he pulled the cut-out. I watched the rider tugging off his gauntlets and entering the tower, glancing over his shoulder at the darkening eastern sky. As I followed the direction of his glance, I caught the movement I had been awaiting on the dispersals to my right. The port outer propellers of two neighbouring bombers were slowly turning, and, as I watched, a blue-grey plume of smoke curled from the exhaust of the nearer aircraft, the propeller-blades turned faster and blurred into invisibility. A second later the sound of the engine reached me, roaring harshly as it started, then settling to a heavy drone. The port inner engine fired in turn, followed by the starboard inner, starboard outer, and now from dispersals all around the airfield came initial roar and subsequent rumble as the bombers came to life.

A small fleet of vehicles was assembling beside the watchtower: fire tenders, two flight vans, an ambulance and a Hillman saloon flying a pennant on the bonnet which I took to identify the Station Commander. Other vehicles were moving on the perimeter track between dispersals, but even those that passed me closely were soundless against the growing clamour of the aircraft engines.

A movement drew my attention to the left. Lancaster PH C for Charlie was lurching slowly out of dispersal, marshalled by an airman walking backwards, beckoning hands above his head. As the bomber swung on to the taxiway, the marshaller turned and ran for the grass, out of the aircraft's path. He stood, holding up his thumbs, as Charlie lumbered past, and then bent over, clasping his cap to his head, as the slipstream of the four propellers washed over him. The Lancaster moved warily along the taxiway, rudders swinging, brakes squealing, and as it passed me I saw the mid-upper gunner's face behind his gun barrels. I put up a thumb and saw his gloved hand wave in reply.

Now all around the darkening airfield the bombers were moving, making the amber taxiway lamps twinkle as they passed between them, forming two processions, one from either side of the main runway, converging on the steady red light that marked the airfield controller's caravan. Between the two processions glowed the flarepath lights.

A green light flickered from the caravan — the leading aircraft moved on to the runway, straightened into wind, paused while the engines cleared their throats, and drove, uncertainly at first and then with gathering momentum, into headlong chase for flight. As it lifted, the next Lancaster was already rolling forward, and then another, until three aircraft moved within my field of vision. The first was slowly climbing to the left, its navigation lights just visible above the tree line, the second running tail-up for take-off, and the third swinging on to the runway by the caravan. The air was becoming filled with heavy noise, which mounted to a peak as each successive bomber passed my vantage point. I put my fingers to my ears, and wondered how much noise the night could hold.

It must have been some six hours later that the first returning bomber wakened me, and I lay in the dark hut listening to the change of key as the airscrews sped to overcome the added drag of the main wheels thrusting from their housings. Then the sound was multiplied as other bombers joined the circuit, and soon the reverberation of their growling engines lulled me back to sleep.

Next morning, starting from the orderly room in the Station Headquarters, we carried our arrival chits hither and thither on the camp, seeking an official signature from every section, in a programmed tour of exploration. Pausing for a cup of tea among a group of aircrew at the NAAFI wagon, I received news of Mugsy Johnson. He was at Ludford Magna, eight miles north-east of Wickenby, flying Lancasters with 101 Squadron. We had first met at the aircrew reception centre in Regent's Park in 1941, and had been together since, throughout our training. This was the first time our paths had led apart. Johnson was a gangling, long-faced Londoner, with a self-dispraising sense of humour. This I liked, and many of his other ways. But I was moved to criticism when he made it his habit, on a freezing training airfield in the wilds of Shropshire, to combat the double threat of the night air and the early morning parade by completely dressing as far as greatcoat and gloves before going to bed. Unfortunately, Johnson combined a strong thirst with a weak bladder, and with a disregard for social convention. My bed was by the window, and my sleep was regularly interrupted by Johnson kneeling heavily across me to piddle into the night.

In the morning, he would stir thirty seconds before "fall-in", take his cap from beneath the pillow, thrust his feet into his boots, and emerge blinking and muttering to take his place on parade.

At Wickenby I met another man who piddled out of a window, but he did it from a Lancaster cockpit window, 18,000 feet above Germany. This was McLaughlin, our deputy flight commander, who, owing to the high mortality rate among his seniors, was more often acting flight commander than deputy. As such, he took me on my first operational mission, to Cologne on 3 July 1943, as his second pilot, in a Mark I Lancaster DV171, K-King.

A tube attached to the control column, venting to atmosphere, was meant to meet the pilot's requirements, but McLaughlin didn't care to use it. On later occasions I learned to share his view; the tube would become blocked by ice at some point in its travel, and the resulting overflow at the input end was unpleasant. Somewhere near Aachen, as I was assimilating a first sight of hostile flak and searchlights, McLaughlin loosened his safety-straps and parachute harness. The roar of the slipstream deepened as he opened his side-window about six inches. Ponderously, deliberately, he turned to the window and set his left knee on the parachute seat. I had no idea what he was doing, and glanced back at the flight engineer for reassurance. Impassive eyes between helmet and oxygen mask told me nothing. I returned, fascinated, to McLaughlin, whose attitude suddenly took on a familiar shape. Holding himself sufficiently far from the window to avoid frostbite or dismemberment, he made use of the slipstream's suction to achieve his purpose.

McLaughlin resumed his seat and strappings. A brilliant yellow light appeared dead ahead and flew straight at us.

"Duck!" said McLaughlin.

Shrapnel pattered on the fuselage. The mid-upper gunner spoke on the intercom.

"Right through my perspex — just missed my head. There's a hell of a draught."

I stared at the sky in front of us. Among the groping searchlight beams, the white and yellow flak bursts formed a sparkling wall. It was hard to believe that we could pass through that unceasing barrage. Was it always like this? Perhaps not; perhaps this was the greatest anti-aircraft barrage ever mustered. Perhaps the enemy had warning of this raid weeks ago, and every gun-battery in Germany had been deployed to defend Cologne.

I looked at McLaughlin. He appeared unexcited, slumped in his seat, hands resting loosely on the control wheel. He grunted placid responses to the bomb-aimer's sing-song chant of guidance:

"Steady . . . steady . . . tracking in nicely."

"Mm-hm."

"Steady . . . bomb-doors open."

"Open."

"Steady . . . left, left . . . steady."

"Mm."

The flickering wall ahead was now also to our right, to our left, above us and below. Parallel lines of tracer bullets made an intermittent winking curve through the darkness. I saw another bomber, exhausts glowing orange, drift across our flight path. Shimmering pulses of light showed the city below as the 4000lb cookies hit the ground. The river gleamed, darkened, and gleamed again.

The bombs dropped. McLaughlin swung the wheel to port as the bomb-doors closed. Gradually the searchlights and the barrage fell behind us. A sense of relief pervaded me; elated phrases bubbled in my thoughts, and I put my hand to the microphone switch on my mask to utter them. I turned to McLaughlin. His posture was unchanged, his eyes looked back serenely, pale blue, slightly bloodshot. I left the mike switch off, the thoughts unspoken, and bent to take the readings on the fuel gauges.

New crews were broken in gently. The pilot usually had his first operational experience as second pilot with a seasoned captain and crew, and his first trip captaining his own crew was often to lay mines in enemy waters. This type of mission was known as "gardening", and the mines were similarly termed "vegetables". Thus I went to Cologne as McLaughlin's second pilot on 3 July, and took my own crew mine-laying three nights later in ED414 Easy Two. The mines weighed 1500lb each, dull cylinders to wallow in the water between the Ile de Re and La Rochelle. We dropped six mines at three-second intervals, heading north at 1000 feet from a lucky G-fix in the Bay of Biscay.

Nobody paid us the smallest attention, and it seemed a piddling mission for the mighty Lanc.

We crowded into the curtained briefing room out of the late afternoon sunlight. A layer of cigarette smoke hung above us, like mist on an autumn morning; through it we stared at the red-ribboned route on the map above the platform.

"Leverkusen, is it?"

"No, the other side of the river. It's Cologne."

"You went there on your second-dicky trip, didn't you, skip?"

"That's right."

"Piece of cake — you know the way there."

"And back."

"Where do we cross the coast?"

We filed into our allotted row of chairs, and augmented the general chatter with our own. I admired the blackboard drawing of the pathfinder technique, under which the legend read: "If target is obscured by cloud bomb sky-markers red dripping green." The rattle of conversation and the foot-shuffling stilled as the authoritative footsteps of the Station Commander and the Squadron Commander beat a tattoo down the centre aisle. The Squadron Commander mounted the platform and turned to face us, clipboard in hand.

"Right, quiet everybody. Captains, answer your names. I want to know if any of your crew are absent, and why. 'A' flight first — Squadron Leader Slade?"

"Sir."

"Flight Lieutenant Rowland?"

As the roll was called, I watched the Station Commander settling into an armchair below the platform. He leafed through the papers on his table, commenting on them in a whisper to the WAAF officer beside him. She was the junior intelligence officer, and known to all as Clueless Kate. A green telephone at the Station Commander's elbow buzzed, and he was still listening to the receiver and scribbling on the blotter when the roll-call ended. The Squadron Commander called for the intelligence briefing, and the senior IO, blackboard-pointer in one hand and pipe in the other, took his place.

"Well, gentlemen, your target tonight is Cologne, on the banks of the Rhine, here."

He jabbed the pointer at the map, where the river writhed through the red-crayoned flak defences.

"Now, Cologne is the centre of trade, traffic and political activity in the Rhine province, and it has a population of 912,000. It's the main railway centre of the Rhineland, and an important inland port. Its position on the river . . ."

My attention wavered. I felt unable to concentrate, like in my schooldays, when I would gaze at the teacher, hearing but not listening, looking at the blackboard when he looked at it, smiling when he smiled, fidgeting when the boy at the next desk fidgeted. Like a mirror: seeing all, reflecting all, retaining nothing.

". . . and its proximity to the coalfields of the Ruhr has encouraged the growth of firms specialising in light and heavy engineering, chemicals and building. We hope that your visit tonight will do something to discourage that growth."

We dutifully murmured our recognition of the sally.

"The chief war factories of Ehrenfeld, Kalk and Mülheim lie to the east of the city, and tonight's attack . . ."

The met man, who had been preparing his slide projector at the back of the room, now crept to his seat in the front row stooping low as though fearful of obscuring, even for an instant, our view of the senior IO.

". . . Wellingtons, Stirlings and Halifaxes. You form part of a force of 156 Lancasters from numbers one and five groups. The Pathfinder Force technique is on the board here . . ."

The senior IO descended carefully from the platform, and approached the blackboard, pointer at the ready.

"Here is your target. This is your last leg into the target, a narrow turn to starboard when your bombs have gone, and your route out. You are primarily to bomb the red target-indicators, shown by these red blobs. If no red TIs are visible, then bomb the centre of the cluster of green backers-up. If cloud conditions prohibit the use of ground-marking methods, the sky-marking will be by red flares dripping green stars."

He tapped the appropriate illustration with his pipe, frowned at the ashes which fell on the floor, exchanged pipe for pointer, and resumed the platform.

"Right. Now, as to defences: most of you visited Cologne on the night of 3 July, only five nights ago, so you know more about them than I can tell you. However, for the benefit of the others I'll read the summary of reports taken from crews at interrogation. Flak was not so heavy as expected, the main opposition being from barrage flak on the run-in to the target; tonight's route should keep you clear of that, and light flak was only slight to moderate. A considerable number of scarecrow flares were employed by the enemy, but I don't believe anyone is going to be worried by these rather amateurish attempts at psychological warfare. Defences *en route* . . ."

I remember Buzz Marshall telling me that he had been severely shaken by his first sight of a scarecrow flare, which had burst a few feet above and in front of him. It had looked for all the world like a PFF kite receiving a direct hit, with TIs and marker flares igniting in a multi-coloured blaze of light. I had asked Buzz how he knew it wasn't an aircraft, and he had said he didn't know — the IO had told them it was a scarecrow at interrogation.

"Now, if anyone should have the misfortune to be forced down in the target area, the best bet would be to make for the French frontier west of Aachen. This part of the frontier is still not heavily guarded, and if you can reach this point on the map under cover of darkness . . ."

We had heard that crews who baled out over the target and descended into the city streets were liable to be summarily dispatched by the more vengeful citizens

— by hanging from a lamp-post or by combustion on the nearest fire.

"Don't forget to empty your pockets before you go and, captains, check that each of your crew has his escape aids and money wallet before you leave the briefing room . . ."

You simply let yourself roll over when you hit the ground; the instructor had told us that it was no worse than jumping off a six-foot wall. You must hide your parachute, bury it if possible, and get as far away from it as you could before daybreak. I thought of the story of the pilot whom the French underground had eventually got out: he had buried his parachute carefully, and travelled like the wind all night, feeling, as he said, the hot breath of the Gestapo on his neck. Just before dawn, he had found a ditch in which to lie low for the day, and, burrowing deep, had come upon his neatly-folded parachute. I giggled at the memory, and the IO frowned at me suspiciously as he took his seat.

The Squadron Commander did not waste words: "Right. Met?"

The met man hastily mounted the platform and, with an anxious air, lowered a white screen over the wall map by manipulating a system of cords and pulleys. The lights were put out, and the disembodied voice of the met man rose above the hum of the projector.

"This is the estimated synoptic situation for 2300hrs tonight. I don't think it's quite in focus — er — could you possibly — ah that's better. As you can see, there's a cold front lying directly across your route, and extending over most of your passage across the North Sea. Base conditions for take-off will be good, however, and you should have practically no cloud at all over the target itself. Base conditions on return . . ."

The slide changed to a diagram of the cloud on our route in cross-section. There was a lot over the North Sea between 2,000 and 20,000 feet, and I wriggled uncomfortably at the thought of all that instrument flying ahead. The met man ended his briefing with surprising theatricality by stepping into his projector's beam and bowing stiffly towards the CO.

"Right. Navigation?"

The nav leader was on leave, and his deputy, a stocky young officer with a fresh complexion and a very battered peaked cap, stepped up.

"Leave the lights out, will you? I want to show you the concentration diagrams for your last trip."

The projector threw an outline of the Dutch coast on the screen. The plot showed where each of the squadron's aircraft was at the time when it should have been crossing the coast on the way to the target. The second plot told a similar story for the route homewards, and it showed a marked deterioration in concentration. The scattered picture inspired the acting nav leader to voice some words of criticism of the navigators concerned, but he was halted by a harsh whisper from Tiny Watson.

"Never mind the inquest — get on with the bloody briefing."

The met man and the flying controller, working as a team, successfully rolled the screen up, and we blinked as the lights came on again.

"Have all navigators got their flimsies? Right, I'll run through the set-course and turning-point times for the first wave. Second wave people add three minutes, third wave add . . ."

The drone of figures set my mind wandering again. Dimly I heard the muted buzz of the CO's telephone, and absently watched him pick up the receiver and hold it to his ear, shading his eyes with the other hand. A sepulchral voice behind me murmured: "Scrub!" but the navigators were bent to their logs until their leader put his clip-board under his arm, and pushed back the sleeve of his tunic:

"Right — check your watches. It's coming up to fourteen minutes to six — ten seconds to go — five seconds — four — three — two — one — now. Seventeen forty-six."

The next to speak was the bombing leader, a fair-moustached and lanky Scotsman, who read quietly from his notes without embellishment or gesture. He told where each bomb was stationed in the bomb-bay, and which switch on the panel should be pressed to let it fall. Each Lancaster would weigh about 63,0001b at take off, and the average bomb load was two 1,000 pounders, one 4,000 pounder, and twelve and two-thirds SBC — the incendiaries. I heard him speak of photo flashes, jettison bars and terminal velocities, but the dry manner of his speech drained his phrases of their drama. My imagination, deep in torpor, failed to open to their meaning.

Larry wrote all down with scowling concentration. He wagged his head portentously at me as the Scotsman sat down, as if to say, "At last, we have had the real import of the briefing."

The signals leader, who appeared anxious to draw as little attention to himself as possible, half rose from his chair and addressed his audience diffidently.

"I should like to see all wireless-operators after the briefing."

Although grateful for his brevity, I was intrigued by his reticence, and made a note to ask Charlie why his leader found it necessary to brief him and his colleagues in private. But the gunnery leader was already talking, hands in pockets, cap at an angle.

"Remember that you gunners are responsible for the safety of your crew from enemy attack the entire time you're in the air. Keep your eyes peeled. Don't narrow your search to one quarter. Swing your turrets round and keep your eyes moving all the time. Watch especially for attacks from under the tail when you're going through the GCI belts, which are marked on the map. Captains can help their gunners here by dipping a wing at regular intervals, so that the mid-upper gunner can search directly underneath. If you are attacked, be prompt and lucid with your evasive action, and keep your captain informed at all times just where the fighter is. As he moves around you, pass him on to whoever's in the best position to watch him. Don't waste ammunition on him while he's out of range, but give him everything you've got if he comes in close. If you're under attack, or you have a fighter under observation, only one gunner should watch him. The other should be looking out for a possible mate for number one. I'm saying all this principally for the benefit of the four new gunners on tonight, and I'd like to see them after the briefing for a few minutes."

He took his hands out of his pockets, and turned towards the Station Commander.

"That's all, sir."

The man from Flying Control, a film actor in peacetime, whose well-known features and bearing brought a Hollywood glitter to the scene, began with instructions about taxiing and a description of the perimeter lighting. He then spoke of the runway.

"From what met has said, it seems we shall be able to use the long runway for take-off, and the wind should be light enough for us to use it all night, although you might have a slight crosswind when you get back. If the wind speed warrants a change of runway, we'll let you know on RT when you rejoin the circuit . . ."

He continued to talk smoothly about diversion airfields for use in the event of a weather clamp on Lincolnshire, about searchlight homing for aircraft in trouble, and about RT procedures.

"I don't need to impress on you the need for strict RT silence before take-off. Leave your eleven-ninety-sixes on stud 'A', base frequency, in case there's an urgent message for you. Join the circuit on return at 2,000 feet or under the cloud-base, whichever is the lower. Call Control and let us know you're back. We'll give you a height to circle at, and then we'll bring you down in 500 feet steps until it's your turn to land. Acknowledge each instruction so we know you're not flying up someone else's tail. When you get 'prepare to land', come down to 1,000 feet, switch your downward ident light on, and position yourself at a reasonable distance behind the aircraft on 'pancake'. Let us know when you're downwind. The aircraft in front of you should be down and close to clearing the runway when you come round to the funnel lights, lined up for landing. Call again there — just say your aircraft letter and 'funnels'. We'll say either pancake, or continue approach, or go round again. When you're down, taxi clear of the runway as soon as you can, and call 'clear'."

There was a ripple of movement over the room as the Station Commander stood up, one hand in his pocket, the other smoothing his black moustache.

"I've been informed that the Wellingtons and Stirlings won't be with you tonight, because of the height of the cloud on the route. I'm sure you all sympathise with them . . ."

His voice sounded fluting and affected after the resonant mid-Atlantic tones of the Flying Control officer. He cocked an eyebrow at the map.

"There's nothing I want to add to what you already know. Your meal was ordered for six o'clock, and it's five past now, so you'd better hurry. Locker-rooms at six-thirty. Good luck."

After a hurried meal, we prepared ourselves for flight. A notice read: "Leave your locker-keys with the NCO i/c locker room."

"What's the idea of that?"

"In case you don't come back, stupid. So they don't have to break the door down to get at your gear."

"Bollocks. I'm coming back. I'll keep the key myself."

As the bombs fell, the fact that I should feel no shock of personal reaction was in itself a sort of shock. Perhaps it was an act of such incalculable violence as to prohibit normal comprehension. My small experience of previous, and far less violent acts had taught me that they bred a sense of guilty self-dislike. So what appalling pang might be aroused by this ferocious deed? But that hollow in my mind remained unfilled, and the need to concentrate on height and speed and heading took command of all my thoughts.

We hung, balanced and steady, in the midst of an expanse of flame-shot havoc. Certainly, the enemy was doing his utmost to destroy us in his turn, to find us with radar and searchlights, to kill us with bullets from his fighters and shells from his guns. That was a physical matter for us, and would be physically resolved. What could not be resolved was the gross imbalance of the scene: the contrast of the bright chaos that seethed four miles below us with the cold, pale readings on my cockpit dials, the flat laconic comments of the crew.

With almost imperceptible progression, we passed across the city of Cologne. I heard the click as Cassidy flicked his microphone switch on:

"Turn starboard on to two-one-five degrees."

The time was twenty past one. Two minutes crept by, and Lanham reported a shattering explosion, emanating from the centre of the concentrated fires which lit the city's heart. He could still see the target's glow when we crossed the frontier into southern Belgium.

Two hours later, having followed the 50th parallel westward to leave the French coast at le Tréport, we passed on our homeward course above Dungeness. As I steered north for Wickenby over the Vale of Kent, I warmed to the thought of flying the world's best heavy bomber, returning for the first time from a German target, cruising home to base above the fields and towns of England. After six hours at the controls, my contact with the aircraft was instinctive and relaxed. We rolled into a turn together, held the turn steadily, without adjustment, with no anxious glances at the dials or searches for the dim horizon. I could scan the sky or talk to the crew, while my senses told me that the turn was accurate. How satisfying it was to fly the Lancaster. These moods of happy mastery were to recur at many times, but balanced by other times when my confidence was harshly shaken, with lapses into sickening self-doubt.

We patrolled the circuit until our turn to land, and I finally set R-Robert, ED972, on the ground at 0437hrs. Back at interrogation, while waiting to report to the intelligence officer, I read again the names of the 12 Squadron captains who had set out for Cologne: Squadron Leader Slade, Flight Lieutenants Burkhardt, McLaughlin, Rowlands and Weeks, Flying Officers

Ashburner, Snell, Wood and Wright, Pilot Officers Gilman and Lawrence, Warrant Officer Smith, Flight Sergeants Brown, Gardiner and Mizon, Sergeants Aspden, Borland, Currie, Fordyce and McMillan. Everyone had come safely home to Wickenby.

Wickenby was now indeed our home, and we accustomed ourselves with the readiness which servicemen must acquire, to the camp's lay-out and environs, its advantages and drawbacks. For a few days in July, there were no cigarettes to be had in the sergeants' mess, and the more devoted tobacco addicts in the crew were reduced to begging from those of their colleagues who had contrived to hoard a packet or two. Charles Fairbairn was one in whom reliance could be placed at such times of need. He was never completely bereft of cigarettes (although he swore that Lanham and I deliberately induced him to take up smoking so that we could borrow from him when we ran out), nor of chewing-gum, chocolate, clean socks, button-polish, shoe-polish, hair-cream, razor-blades, nor of any other minor domestic requirement. A couple of days before a pay-day, when the rest of the crew were penniless, Fairbairn's resources were adequate, not only for his own needs, but to provide small loans to others. These he furnished patiently, without protest or patronage. He didn't exhort us to follow his prudent example, but simply bestowed ten shillings here, a pound there, with a whimsical smile creasing his long, kindly face. After pay-day the procedure was "so much for Fairbairn, and the remainder for me." The cherubic Protheroe, who was developing a taste for strong drink and weak

WAAFs, but had yet to discover his gift for making a steady income from the game of shoot-pontoon, found it best to pass his entire pay-packet to Fairbairn and draw on it as needed during the following fortnight.

Larry Myring, away from the importunate Freda, spent his pay on Meux's ale, and frequently applied himself so earnestly to its consumption as to achieve a state of incoherent, giggling paralysis by closing time. Lanham viewed such excesses with disdain.

"He's grog-happy, our Larry. I'm glad my neck doesn't depend on his reactions."

While Myring devoted his spare time to the local ales, and Protheroe to his convivial girls, Cassidy and I had few opportunities to pursue our mutual interest in cricket. When, on 17 July, the sergeants played a match against the officers on the bumpy station pitch, it was a rare event, for there were seldom enough of us available to make up two elevens. We had the moon to thank for our sport on this occasion, for it was almost full, and gave so much advantage to the German night-fighters that we were stood down until it waned. Instead of operations, some night-flying practice had been arranged, and the match had to end at six o'clock. Jim Cassidy played for the officers, and bowled accurately at medium pace, with a slinging action from a short, crab-like run. Fast bowling presented alternate threats to batsmen's shoulders and ankles, as it flew unpredictably from the uneven turf. Only the Station Commander, Group Captain Crummy, had the required technique — straight bat, left elbow up, head over the line of the ball — to overcome the conditions.

Once he had succumbed to a horrid shooter, the other batsmen offered little resistance, and the sergeants would have won the day if we had not been obliged to draw stumps for flying.

As captain of the sergeants' team, I rubbed it well in to Cassidy that we had enjoyed the better of the match, which he ungrudgingly admitted. I knew he would; he had to be honest. That was one of the facets on the diamond of his character which I had seen in his eyes when we met. Since then, I had seen other sides, and one at least had the glint of old-fashioned puritanism. No matter how rude the blows of fate, Jimmy never permitted himself the common outlet of bad language, and this was remarkable in view of the average Australian's proclivity for swearing. Some of them would interject a "bloody" between every other word of a sentence, and they even had a song to exemplify this tendency, of which the first verse ran:

This bloody town's a bloody cuss,
No bloody pubs, no bloody bus,
Nobody cares for bloody us,
Oh, bloody, bloody, bloody!

Perhaps out of respect for Cassidy's feelings, we made an effort to expurgate our language. For a few days in August, we administered a system of fines, ranging from a penny for each four-letter word, through twopence for obscene gestures and threepence for more subtle verbal variations, to fourpence for downright blasphemy. Unfortunately, we found that determining who said what invoked more foul language than ever, and gave the system up by mutual consent. The score sheet read: Protheroe tenpence, Myring one shilling and a penny, Walker nil, Fairbairn threepence, Lanham one and sevenpence, Currie one and fourpence. It was generally agreed that Myring had been let off lightly, as his record included one sentence in which he had employed every vile term known to man, with some unheard-of combinations, for which he had merely been fined a nominal sixpence.

We had an example of Cassidy's reaction to adversity on Friday, 9 July, when we flew LM321 Howe Two to Gelsenkirchen in the Ruhr. We took off at 11.15p.m. with a 4000lb cookie, two 1000 pounders and the incendiary canisters. We crossed the northern margin of the Zuider Zee, and then turned starboard for the Ruhr. We bombed the target on a southerly heading, passed between Essen and Bochum, and continued south beyond Cologne. I did my utmost to ignore the formidable defences as we made the bombing run, but when the bombs had fallen I was glad to concentrate on avoiding the searchlights and flak barrage. Cassidy, blind to the excitement at his curtained desk, picked a moment when my sweat was running freely to enquire:

"Nav to pilot. What's the air temperature?"

"Bloody hot."

"Eh? Aw, don't give us the creeps, Jack. I need it for the log."

"In a minute, Jim."

Gradually the tumult died away behind us. Lanham, looking aft from the rear turret, whistled a tune of the times.

"That's what the flak reminds me of, Jack. 'Stairway to the stars'."

We lost the use of the airspeed indicator at about two o'clock in the morning, over the Ardennes. This was a deprivation I had not known before, and I took a long time to get accustomed to it. The sequence of my routine search around the panel continued to include the useless dial, and every time I wasted seconds boggling at the misplaced pointer, and gripped the wheel, forestalling nothing.

As we flew across the channel, dropping down to Dungeness, the warming atmosphere de-iced the tube, and allowed the rushing air to indicate a truthful reading. We reached the environs of Lincoln later than we should, and Wickenby eluded Cassidy's best attempts to find it. None of us had been in the air for so long before; fatigue and inexperience combined to thwart his search. The G-box lattice lines led us a weary dance, as Robin Goodfellow misled the midsummer night's wanderers. At last I found an airfield and set Howe Two down. I pulled up outside the watchtower, and an airman emerged. Lanham spoke to him from the rear door.

"What airfield is this?"

"Eh?"

"Where are we?"

"What do you want to know for?"

"Because we're bloody lost!"

"Oh. Can I see your identity card?"

"Get stuffed. What d'you think we are — the flaming Luftwaffe?"

"No, but . . ."

"Look, we're from 12 Squadron. We're on ops."

"Oh."

A staff car arrived, carrying an officer, wearing a greatcoat and flying-boots over his pyjamas. Lanham came through on the intercom.

"We're at Fiskerton, Jack. Their CO's here — wants to know if there's anything he can do."

"Thanks, Charlie. Okay, navigator?"

"Yeah. It's only seven miles from base — we can map-read now it's getting light."

Walker was tapping the fuel gauges and frowning.

"We're very low on fuel, skip."

"I only want five minutes. Let's go."

I waved to Fiskerton's CO, who stood at the salute as Howe Two moved away. We reached Wickenby at quarter to six, with Cassidy still muttering apologies. It touched me to see how savagely he blamed himself.

After the Gelsenkirchen mission we had a break from Wickenby. The leave allowance for bomber crews was six days every six weeks, and our first leave away from camp was due. Lanham and I travelled south together, he to stay with relatives at Leytonstone, I to my parents' home in Harrow. Among the visits I made during the week, one, at my mother's firm suggestion, was to the headmaster of my old school. When I had paid him my respects, he took me to the common room for coffee, and I had a few words with other of my former masters. The teacher who was responsible for the Air Training Corps cadets suggested that I should attend one of their training sessions, and give the boys a lecture on Lancaster operations. I didn't care for the idea.

"Oh, no. I'm not a lecturer."

"All quite informal, you know."

"Yes, but . . ."

They'd love to see you."

"Well, I could come along and have a chat, if you like. And I'll see if I can get my rear gunner to give me moral support."

"That would be splendid."

Lanham didn't take much persuading. He mounted the rostrum in the crowded classroom with a bound, perched on the table and, swinging his legs, beamed at the silent youths.

"Some of you may be wondering why I'm wearing a different coloured uniform from the skipper. It's because I'm an Australian, and our sky's a nice, bright blue — not grey like yours. As Jack said, I'm his rear gunner. I fly in the turret at the tail end, about the length of a cricket pitch from where he sits. He relies a lot on me and the navigator, 'cause the nav tells him where we're going, and I tell him where we've been. We've got another two turrets, as well as mine: one in the nose, and one on top of the fuselage . . ."

A thin arm, with corporal's tapes on its sleeve, was raised in the front row.

"Excuse me, sir, may I ask a question?"

"Sure. And I'm not a 'sir', I'm a sergeant. But you can call me Charlie, if you like."

"Thank you, sir — I mean, Charlie. Is it correct that your guns are the same calibre as the soldiers' rifles in the last war?"

Charlie grinned, and nodded.

"Yeah, that's true enough. They're Browning .303 machine-guns, but don't forget I've got four of them, and the front turret's got two. So has the mid-upper."

Another boy put up a hand.

"Please, sir, how do yours compare with the guns on the night-fighters?"

"Not too well for size. The Messerschmitt 110 has four cannons, the 109 has three and a couple of machine-guns, and the Focke Wulf 190 has four 20mm cannons plus two machine-guns. But we're not supposed to go looking for shoot-outs with the Jerry fighters; we reckon to try and dodge them. Our guns are okay, once they get in close."

The first boy, who looked like a half-size Heinrich Himmler in his glinting, steel-rimmed spectacles, returned to the attack.

"It's correct, isn't it, that the American bombers are better armed than ours?"

"Too right. The Forts have twelve .5 machine-guns. They also have a whole lot of armour-plating, which we haven't, but I reckon they need all the protection they can get on their daylight raids, and, of course, they don't lift anything like the bomb load we do. The skipper sings a song about that, don't you Jack?"

I obliged with a verse, to the tune of "John Brown's body".

We can fly a Flying Fortress up to forty thousand
    feet,
We can fly a Flying Fortress up to forty thousand
    feet,
We can fly a Flying Fortress up to forty thousand
    feet,
But we only carry a teeny, weeny bomb!

During the polite murmur of amusement which followed this, Lanham produced some cardboard silhouettes, borrowed from the gunnery section at Wickenby.

"Okay, let's see what you guys are like on aircraft recognition."

The boys responded with instant accuracy to such routine shapes as the Douglas Boston, the Bristol Beaufort, the Republic Thunderbolt, and the Lockheed Lightning. They dealt devastatingly with such posers as the Martin Mariner, the Junker 290, the Curtiss Helldiver and the Heinkel 177. Even the esoteric shadows of the Fiat G50, the Piper Grasshopper and the Arado 196 failed to halt their fluent progress. I was glad I wasn't in competition with them, and that I was free to make escape from the earnest embryonic airmen, down Harrow Hill to meet sweet-smiling Joan, in whose soft arms I had engaged to falter round a dance floor later in the evening. The six-piece band, cool in white slacks and pale-blue yachting blazers, pounded and blew the dance tunes of the moment: "That Old Black Magic", "Surrey with the Fringe on Top", "My Lovely Russian Rose", and, inevitably, "Roll out the Barrel". The drummer was an old acquaintance and at his suggestion, the leader called on me to sing. Having swallowed a glass of brown ale for self-encouragement and lubrication, I gave my pale impersonation of Bing Crosby's "Stardust".

Joan stretched her steps to match my stride as we walked arm in arm through the blacked-out streets, which still felt warm from the sunshine of the day. Dancing had brightened her eyes and heightened her colour, and as we walked she babbled happily, her hair tantalising my cheek as she bent her head towards me. Low behind the music of her chatter, I distinguished the unrhythmic murmur of a twin-engined aircraft, flying with rpm unsynchronised. It was coming from the east and getting nearer. The usual air-raid warning had sounded earlier in the evening, and the sound of gunfire had occasionally accompanied the band.

We looked towards the unseen aircraft, and then we heard the whistle, starting on a thin, high note, running down the scale and swelling in volume as the missile fell. Joan's soft voice had halted abruptly, and now she threw herself down on the pavement, pillowing her face on her coat-sleeve. I looked down at her and noticed that her long, smooth hair had swept forward, and lay across her forearm like a matador's cape. I wondered whether I should follow her example, but the piercing whistle reached its nadir, and the fallen object clattered on the asphalt of the tennis court beside us. I guessed it must have been a chunk of shrapnel with a hole in it which made it whistle, or perhaps the nosevane of a bomb. I helped Joan to her feet. She tossed her head, and the mane of hair resettled on her shoulders.

"Gosh, how did you know it wasn't a bomb?"

I shrugged nonchalantly, and bluffed it out.

"You get to know these things when you're on bombers."

CHAPTER
THREE

Hamburg

Hamburg had taken a terrible pounding while we were enjoying our first leave from Wickenby at the end of July. We returned in time to help deliver the final blow on Monday, 2 August. We started DV190 Baker Two's engines at 11.30p.m., and took off twenty minutes later. We circled base on the climb, and emerged into a clear sky at about 9,000 feet, setting course for Mablethorpe twenty-five minutes after midnight. An hour and ten minutes later we were thirty miles west of Heligoland and in trouble. The port outer engine was giving no power, the airspeed indicator had iced up, and the 19,000 feet of altitude that we had struggled to attain were steadily slipping away. Paths became more difficult to find between the towering thunderclouds that had built up over the North Sea, and whenever the turbulent masses closed about us Baker Two took on more ice and fell another couple of hundred feet.

Johnny Walker left the cabin and crawled aft. The Command's new tactic to confuse the enemy radar was the use of "window", thin strips of metal foil, and Walker's chilly task was to drop them through the flare chute in the dark and shaking fuselage. Fairbairn left his radio compartment to assist, remarking as he went, with his usual regard for accuracy, that ice on the aerials had increased their diameter from three-sixteenths of an inch to one and a half inches, and was still growing.

We plunged on south-east for thirty minutes, as hail beat harshly on the canopy, and mauve light flickered about the aerials and front guns. Vivid stabs of lightning opened sudden gorges in the sky, then swirling vapour wrapped us round again. I felt the ice begin to grip the aircraft, now losing height more rapidly. I spoke to the navigator.

"Where are we, Jimmy?"

"Should be about twenty miles south of the target, but I haven't had a fix for some time. Can you see any flares?"

"Can't see anything but cumulo-nimbus."

The bombs fell into the storm from 14,000 feet. Baker Two leaped at their release and settled into a slow and lurching climb. At 18,000 feet we broke into a shaft of clear air as lightning played among the looming anvil-headed clouds. Then the guns found us, and the aircraft shook and rattled as the shells burst close. As I turned to miss them, the cloud enveloped us again, and now its icy grip became like iron. Within seconds, the thirty-ton bomber was a toy for the storm to play with, the wheel locked, immobile as a rock. Baker Two was out of my control.

I could see nothing through the window, nothing but a blue infernal glow. I heard no engines, only roaring wind and savage thunder-claps. For the first time in the air, I felt impotence and, with that, a sudden prick of panic. There was nothing I could do — and yet surely I must do something. I held the wheel, watched the instruments, and waited for a clue to action. The instruments belied each other: no airspeed, but climbing fast.

I felt the stall. The harness straps were pressing hard on my shoulders, my legs were light, loose objects fell about the cabin. Was I hanging in my harness upside-down, or was the aircraft falling faster than my weight? I tried to reject the evidence of the whirling gyro-controlled instruments and to believe the others, which showed nose down, a spin to port, and mounting speed. The ASI had left its ice-bound stop, and was swinging round the dial a second time.

"Pilot to crew, prepare to abandon aircraft — prepare to abandon."

I tried to judge the rate of our descent, and chose 8,000 feet as the height where I must tell the crew to jump. They had to get the hatches open, and push themselves into the roaring slipstream, and still leave time for me to follow, before we fell too low to give the silken canopies time to open.

I don't know whether Baker Two or I recovered from the spin, but now there was only the tearing rush of wind, and the steady movement clockwise of the ASI. The needle made a second circuit of the dial, and verged upon the limit of its travel at 400 miles per hour. If the pitot head were free of ice, so might be the elevators; I pulled back on the wheel with all my strength, as the altimeter read 10,000 feet. At 9,000 feet, the wheel jerked violently in my hands, still I pulled and slowly felt my weight increase, and press into the seat, as the diving angle decreased. Briefly, we emerged below the cloud base, and shot up into it again as I struggled with the wheel.

At last, I found a level attitude at 8,000 feet, and brought the ASI back into the realm of reason. But there was something badly wrong: the wheel, although answering my back- and forward pressures to climb or dive, wagged loosely left and right without response from either aileron to bank and turn. I wondered if the control cables had snapped — that might have been the violent tremor of the wheel. I pushed the rudders alternately, and Baker Two yawed gently in reply.

"Okay, I've got some control now. Let's have an intercom check — rear-gunner?"

No reply from Charlie Lanham.

"Mid-upper?"

"Mid-upper okay, skipper."

"Engineer?"

No answer from Johnny Walker.

"Wireless-operator?"

"Wireless-op strength nine."

"Any idea what's happened to Johnny?"

"Last time I saw him, we were both floating up and down the fuselage like a brace of pheasants on the glorious twelfth."

"Okay, Charlie, go back and see if you can find him. And check the rear-gunner, too."

"Wireless-op going off intercom."

Fairbairn's microphone clicked off, and I continued with the rollcall.

"Navigator?"

"Navigator loud and clear."

"Bomb-aimer?"

"Bomb-aimer okay, skip."

Cassidy could hardly wait for the bomb-aimer to reply, before he called.

"What course are you on?"

I spun the compass dial.

"210 magnetic."

"You're heading straight for Bremen. Turn on to 330."

"330. I'll try."

"Mid-upper to skipper. A bloody great piece of your starboard wing's missing — did you know? Jesus, the port wing's the same!"

"Thanks, George."

So that was it. Both ailerons had been torn off in that screaming, spinning dive. I pushed the starboard rudder, and Baker Two veered right for a few degrees, wings level, then swung back as I released the pressure on the rudder. I tried again, held the pressure on, and pulled the wheel back slightly. A slow, slithering turn developed. Halfway round, I remembered the rotary potential of the engines — the port outer, free of ice, was running smoothly. Playing with the throttle, I let the Merlin bring the port wing up, and Baker Two settled into a steady, balanced turn.

A familiar "puff-puff" in my earphones indicated that Fairbairn was checking his microphone before venturing an utterance.

"Wireless-op here, Jack. I can't find any sign of Johnny, I'm afraid. The main door's open — he might have fallen out. Or jumped. There's a terrible mess down here — 'window' all over the place. The rear-gunner's in his turret."

Myring chimed in from the nose compartment.

"I'll have a look for the engineer, skip. I want to go to the Elsan, anyway."

"Go ahead, Larry. Better get back to your set, Charlie. Pilot to rear-gunner?"

"Rear-gunner, Jack."

"Where were you?"

"I got out to find my 'chute. I sat on the doorstep while you were bringing her down . . ."

I liked that; she was bringing me down. Lanham continued:

". . . the whole kite was covered in St Elmo's fire — ice all over the wings — really a marvellous sight."

"I'm glad you enjoyed it. Did you see anything of the engineer?"

"You can't see anything in the fuselage. There's 'window' and stuff everywhere. Shall I . . ."

Protheroe interrupted.

"Mid-upper to skipper."

"Go ahead, George."

"I thought the rear-gunner ought to know — I shan't be able to fire my guns. The interrupter gear's gone unserviceable. I think something broke off in the spin. Shall I get out and look for Johnny?"

"No — leave that to Larry. Stay in the turret and keep your eyes peeled."

"Wireless-op here, Jack. I've been checking the external aerials, and there aren't any. I guess they blew off."

"Bad luck."

I flew on, holding Baker Two just below the cloud-base, at 8,000 feet. When Myring called from the fuselage, he was panting, and I could hear the sound of the slipstream behind his voice.

"I've found the engineer, skip. Buried in bloody 'window'. He's out cold — I think he's banged his nut."

"Is he on oxygen?"

"Yep. That's why I don't want to take his helmet off to look at his head. I'm going to put him on the rest-bed. I'll be off Intercom for a few minutes."

"Right."

We crossed the coast near Bremerhaven at ten minutes to three. Ten minutes later, a searchlight waved towards us from the right, groped closer, and swept the starboard wing. Two more lights from straight below joined the first, and crept along its beam to find us. The flashing stars of flak began to twinkle round us, and I played what evasive games I could with engines, rudders and elevators. I looked for clouds, but they had disappeared. I spoke to Jimmy.

"We're in some defences, nav."

"Ah, goodoh, Jack, that'll be Heligoland. I've been waiting for a fix. Let me know when it's right underneath, will you?"

"Oh, sure."

But now, miraculously, the flak dwindled, and the last two searchlight beams climbed higher up the ladder of the first. I looked up, and there on the port beam, 5,000 feet above us, cruised another Lancaster, majestic, straight and level. The searchlights settled on her, the twinkling flak shells clustered, but she passed on oblivious, like Oberon's imperial votaress.

"Mid-upper here, skipper. What d'you think of that bugger at ten o'clock high? They must all be asleep!"

I was glad when another drift of cloud hid the sacrifice from my view. The feeling came that Baker Two and we were leading charmed lives that August night, and it was with a degree of confident abandon that, five minutes later, I threw her into steep corkscrew turns to evade a prowling fighter.

At 3.30 we turned west-south-west, with 400 miles to go for Mablethorpe. I began to consider how I might make a landing. I had heard no precedent for a Lancaster landing without aileron control, but in my present mood I couldn't think it impracticable, not that night. Larry shattered my euphoria when he returned from nursing Johnny. Crouching beside me, his eyes squinting with alarm, he growled:

"Cripes, Jack, we're bloody short of petrol. These tanks are damn near empty — we'll never make the coast."

"They should be half full. How's Johnny?"

"He's conscious, but I reckon he's got concussion."

"Pilot to engineer. I need you here to check the fuel. Go and give him a hand, will you, Larry?"

Walker reached the cabin, white-faced and pale-lipped, but with enough sense to get the true readings from the fuel gauges. Charlie Lanham cackled from the rear turret.

"Duff gen, Myring!"

Larry crept down into the nose muttering.

Walker was slumped against the starboard cabin window, fumbling at the intercom switch on his mask. I leaned over to turn it off for him, and looked into his eyes. They seemed unfocused, and his face was drained of blood. I told him to go back to the rest-bed, but he didn't move, and the wireless operator had to take him aft. When Fairbairn reported that he had made the engineer comfortable, and checked that he was breathing oxygen, Lanham's voice came through my headphones:

"Pilot from rear-gunner. Do you reckon we're clear of fighters?"

"I don't know. I should think so. Why?"

"I'll come up and take Johnny's place. Give you a hand."

It crossed my mind that he might be feeling lonely in the cold extremity of Baker Two's tail-end, or that he had decided that I could use some close moral support. Either way, it would be good to have him by my side.

"Okay, rear-gunner, you're clear to leave the turret."

Lanham appeared in the cabin a few moments later, and perched on the engineer's bench seat. Crawling up the fuselage in his heavy suit had brought him out in a sweat. He wiped the back of his gauntlet across his face, then folded his arms and stared ahead into the darkness. His gravely alert expression was exactly suited to the situation, but it made me want to make him laugh. I nudged him with my elbow, and waggled the useless control wheel loosely with my fingertips. I spun it round from left to right, and back again, grinning at Lanham. He looked worried for a moment, staring at the wheel and back at me, then I saw the gleam of his teeth as he laughed. There wasn't really much to laugh about, but the atmosphere was getting too serious; it needed some of the gravity taken out of it. Lanham settled himself more comfortably, and passed me a pellet of chewing-gum. He stayed beside me for an hour or so while Baker Two flew on westward, sometimes side-slipping a little when I picked up a wandering wing too harshly with the rudders, but on the whole making good her course.

High above the Lincolnshire coast I brought the speed back, put the wheels down, and tried a rate-one ninety-degree turn to port. I couldn't get any flap down — presumably another system had fractured there — and that meant that I must make a long down-wind leg, a shallow approach, and add ten mph on to the landing speed. I practised it at 4,000 feet, and brought Baker Two to the point of the stall. The rudder control was good, but I couldn't manipulate the throttles fast enough to keep the wings level. It would have to be a very straight approach.

"Pilot to crew. The landing may be a bit difficult. You'd better bale out."

There was silence for a few seconds, then Lanham called:

"What are you going to do, Jack?"

"I'm going to put her down at base. But I might make a balls of it."

"You won't. This is your lucky night. I'm staying on board."

I warned them again, but nobody would go. We reached Wickenby five minutes later than the time on our flight plan, and the circuit was clear. I flew parallel with the runway, flashing dash-dot-dot-dot dot-dot-dash-dash-dash on the downward identification-light. A green Very cartridge puffed up from the caravan. I made an accurate approach, but half a mile from touchdown I began to doubt the wisdom of my decision to land her. The way the wings were dipping, left to right and back to the left, was much worse than it had seemed at 4,000 feet. However, there was a rhythm in their rolling movement, and, picking the instant in mid-roll when the wings were level, I banged the main wheels down on the runway and held them there. Baker Two pulled up, squealing, in the last few feet of concrete. It was twenty-seven minutes past five.

The muscles of my legs were tired from the unusual exercise of kicking Baker Two's rudders for three hours, and it was some time before I could stand without support. The crew were less boisterous than usual, oddly gentle as they helped me to get into the crew bus, and had Walker taken to the sick-bay. When we reached the briefing room, the Station Commander strolled towards me as I took a mug of cocoa from the padre's serving-hatch.

"Not one of your better landings, Currie."

"No, sir. If I'd known you were watching I'd have tried harder."

He smiled and started to turn away, but Myring stopped him. "The skipper was in difficulties, sir. He did bloody well to get it down at all."

"Oh? What difficulties were you in, Currie?"

"I hadn't any aileron control, sir. And no flaps."

"Why didn't you have aileron control?"

Mentally, I cursed Larry's intervention. I had hoped to report the incident in my own time to the debriefing officer, with a cigarette to smoke and my feet under the table, and let it go through the normal channels. Now here was the Station Commander staring at me imperiously, one eyebrow raised. The Squadron Commander was at his elbow, and other officers were edging closer. I hadn't had time to sip my cocoa.

"I'm afraid they broke off, sir."

"Broke off? Are you serious, Currie?"

"Yes, sir. We got in a spin, in some cumulo-nimbus near the target."

"I see."

He looked at me quizzically for a moment, then beckoned to the Squadron Commander and walked out to his car. I turned to the crew.

"I don't think he believed me."

"He'll get a shock when he sees the kite, then."

That was the first of several inspections to be undergone by Baker Two, as expert and lay examiners looked at her damaged surface areas, sprung rivets and gaping wings. Meanwhile, T called at the sick-bay to see the damaged Walker, who gave a pallid smile of recognition. The MO said he had concussion, confirming Myring's diagnosis, and that he would be moved to hospital in a few hours' time. I trudged back to the hut.

I felt slightly aggrieved when I was required to report to the Squadron Commander a few hours later, while the rest of the crew slumbered on. Woody gave me a chair in his office, and he sat at his desk making notes while I told him what had happened to Baker Two. When I had finished, he looked up with a smile.

"Well, I think it was a magnificent show. Has it shaken you up a bit?"

"No, I don't think so, sir. We're all fine, except for the engineer. He's gone into Rauceby."

"Would you like to take a few days' leave?"

I considered the kindly suggestion. We had returned from our last leave on Friday night, and this was Tuesday. The state of our finances varied from poor to very poor. Even Fairbairn's fabulous wealth could be measured in terms of shillings, and I decided that more time off would only be an embarrassment.

"No, thank you, sir. I think we'd better get on with the tour." His smile almost became a grin.

"Had enough leave for a while, hm?"

"That's right, sir."

I was pleasantly surprised by the reactions of my colleagues on the squadron, some humorous, all generous. It was good to realise that each could emerge from his own embattled world to remark and applaud another's fortune. But, putting personal thoughts aside, the raid had not been a success. Nature, more terrible and more effective than all man-made defences, had thrown her arms around the city and its ravaged streets and protected it from further horrors. Twenty-five of us had taken off from Wickenby; four thought that they had bombed the target, eight had bombed on ETA, not altogether certain where they were, six had been unable to reach Hamburg and had bombed some other town, three had jettisoned the bomb load in the sea, three had given up the sortie, and one did not return.

CHAPTER
FOUR

Summertime Targets

Walker was still in hospital when we went to Mannheim a week later in DV200 Fox Two. The mishap that had caused his concussion on the Hamburg mission had a further effect: in future, the "window" was to be scattered from the nose instead of from the flare chute at the rear, and the task of dissemination was re-allocated to the bomb-aimer. Larry viewed the modification with disfavour.

"Bloody hell. I drop the bombs, do the map-reading, man the front-turret, and now I've got to push the bloody window out. If you stick a broom-handle up my arse, I'll sweep the cabin floor as well."

In Johnny's absence, we took a stand-in engineer, and at times it was a shock to remember that I had a stranger at my side, who required translations of the signs and nods with which Walker and I were accustomed to communicate.

The six-hour trip, through cloudless skies, passed without alarm. Carrying a cookie, three 1,000 pounders, and thirteen canisters of incendiaries, we took Fox Two above the gleaming Thames to Beachy Head, across the Channel to Boulogne, and east on one long leg to Mannheim, where the Neckar joins the Rhine.

Looking through the navigator's bag for a pencil, I found a couple of brown paper sick-bags. I asked Cassidy why he carried them, and he wriggled uncomfortably.

"Aw, just in case I feel crook some time. A man ought to be prepared for anything!"

Fairbairn had heard the conversation, and later he confirmed what I suspected.

"Jim wouldn't thank me for telling you this, but he has a good sick on every trip. Usually just after take-off, and sometimes later, on evasive action or when it's really bumpy. He's ever so neat about it — never makes a mess."

I took the next opportunity to revive the subject with Cassidy, and to enquire whether it was my occasional rough handling of the aircraft that upset him. He grinned, and shook his head.

"It's not that at all. I was sick on every flight, all through training. It's just a thing I've learned to live with."

"Have you talked to the MO about it?"

"Ah, cripes, Jack, forget it. I'm okay, honestly. It's just nerves, I reckon. Look, I haven't got you lost yet, have I? Well, only once."

I knew the little navigator, for all his smiling modesty, was an immensely determined person, so I said no more. It worried me to think of him, vomiting into his secret paper bags on every mission, but I decided that I would rather fly with a sickly Jimmy than any other navigator, no matter how robust. I did as he asked, and let it drop.

Now came two sorties to Milan, more than eight hours long and rather monotonous, which nevertheless made a welcome break from the steady assault on Germany. On the first attack, which was launched on Thursday, 12 August, we had difficulty in persuading Fox Two to start. The last permitted time for takeoff had long passed when, ignoring the deadline without reaction from the tower, we got her into the air.

We chased the rest of the squadron south-east over France, past Vichy and across the Rhône, keeping south of Switzerland where street lights were burning, nudging the white shoulder of Mont Blanc, brilliant in the moonlight. We had caught up with the stream as we left the Alps behind, to find Milan, lying in a confluence of railways, sleeping on the Lombardy plain.

As we approached, there was every sign of defiance from the city, with searchlights waving energetically and a storm of barrage flak. But as the bombs began to fall all changed: the lights stood still, the flak guns ceased to fire. It was as though a spell had fallen on Milan, and placed its defenders in a passive trance.

We were often in greater danger from the gunfire of our friends than we had been from that of the Italians. The guns of little ships would shoot at us as we neared the English coast, and I never knew whether to switch our lights on to show that we were harmless, or leave them off so as not to make a better target. Sometimes our coastal anti-aircraft batteries would decide that they didn't like Lancasters, and then we had to answer with the colours of the day, shot by Very pistol, if only we could remember what they were. To fire the wrong colours could be more dangerous than to fire none at all. On this occasion we were easing our way across the Channel, a few miles north-west of Le Havre, and aiming for Selsey Bill. Fairbairn was standing beside his radio compartment, looking through the perspex astrodome.

"Wireless-op to skipper. Aircraft flying a parallel course on the starboard beam. I think it's a Lanc."

I was letting "George", the automatic pilot, fly the aircraft, as I sometimes did when we were over water or neutral territory, to ease the purely physical burden of the flight. Now I pulled the lever that released the auto pilot's clutch, and took the wheel.

"Okay, Charlie, keep an eye on him. I don't want him to get too close."

"He's firing at something — it must be something near us. Hey, he's firing at us!"

The lifted starboard wing hid the trigger happy bomber from my view as I sheered smartly off to port.

"Where is he, Charlie?"

"I don't know, Jack. I lost him when you turned, and now I can't find him."

Protheroe spoke soothingly.

"It's okay, skipper. He's high on the starboard quarter about a thousand yards. I'd have shot him up if I'd thought he was going to hit us."

"Oh, good."

Three nights later we went to Milan again, travelling the same route, this time in ED424 Easy Two. It had become my habit to defecate some time between the flying-meal and takeoff, and my state of mind about the mission would be reflected in the consistency of the stool. Judged by this psychosomatic forecast, the second Milan sortie was to be of minimal excitement. It came as something of a shock when the defences of the city, recovered from their previous petrifaction, resisted bravely throughout the attack. We bombed from 20,000 feet at ten minutes past midnight, heading 120° magnetic with the airspeed indicator showing 155mph. Lanham commented:

"I reckon they've had some Jerry gunners posted down here since last time we came."

Cruising home above the high Savoy, we came upon a lonely Alpine gunner, who fired a savage stream of tracer bullets which faded, spent, before they reached our height. The warmth of his futile fusillade was such a contrast with the barren chill of his emplacement, that we recalled him with amusement ever after.

Lanham and I met in London during one of our short periods of leave. We lunched at Australia House, then caught the train to Maidenhead. We stayed at Skindles, on the Thames, took a rowing-boat on the river, laughed, and sang, and played the fool. Lanham performed his impersonation of the comic actor, W. C. Fields, selecting a golf-club from an imaginary bag. He swung the club with ponderous nonchalance, frowned, and solemnly intoned:

"Too heavy."

He cast the club aside, and took another.

"Too light."

And yet a third.

"Too medium."

Later that evening, I discovered the rear-gunner in ferocious argument with an American naval officer, and intervened before they came to blows.

"Come on, Charlie, let's not be nasty to our gallant allies."

His hot glare soon cooled, and he strutted off with me to chatter with the barman. At least another forty-eight hours must pass before we had to fly again, so he permitted me some beer, without revilement, while he allowed himself a grapefruit juice.

The next day, I played for my Old Boys' cricket team, whose organisers usually contrived to find a place for members home on leave. While I fielded, Lanham strolled about the ground, chest thrown out and hands in pockets, stopping for a friendly chat with each occasional spectator. After tea, we built a bomber fuselage from benches and deckchairs. The heavy roller was a "cookie", and Lanham had cricket bats for guns. We parodied a bombing run, which ended when the aircraft tried to fly backwards and the fuselage disintegrated. When stumps were drawn, and I had changed, we took the Metropolitan Line to London, where Lanham had arranged a date.

"I called this Sheila, and she's going to meet us at the pub. We'll pick her cobber up later."

She walked into the hotel bedroom in Sloane Square, swinging her wide hips and her long, coarse hair. Lanham introduced us, and her soft, cool fingers rested in my hand. She raised her pencilled eyebrows and looked me up and down, still undulating slowly.

"So you're his skipper, that I've heard too much about. Okay, let's see you skipper something, like a drink maybe?"

"What will you have?"

"A fainting fit if I don't sit down soon. And Scotch on the rocks, skipper."

I stood aside, or she would have walked through me on her way to the easy chair. A wave of perfumed air washed over me as she swept past. I perched on a bed and looked at her, noticing how closely her costume fitted her, and how white her little teeth showed against the scarlet of her lips.

"Charlie tells me you're a singer."

"Charlie'll tell you anything."

"Sing us a song."

"For my supper?"

"Just for fun. I'd like to hear you."

"What's your favourite, skipper?"

" 'Yours'."

"No, not mine. Your favourite."

"You know what I mean. Don't you like Vera Lynn?"

"Please, skipper. I'm not that kind of girl."

"What kind of girl have you arranged for me this evening?"

"Carole? She's for tail-end Charlie. I'm up front with you."

I glanced warily at the rear-gunner, but he was grinning happily.

"What'd I tell you, Jack? Isn't she a beaut? Come on, let's hit the town!"

On Tuesday, 17 August, the target was a secret experimental station on an island off the southern Baltic coast. At the briefing, the Intelligence Officer told us that the enemy was developing a new generation of radar-controlled night-fighters there, at a place called Peenemunde. We were to go in full moonlight, which we usually avoided, and we were to bomb from an altitude which was under half our normal bombing height, because the target had to be accurately pinpointed. If we failed to knock Peenemunde out at the first try, we would have to go again the next night, and so on until it was flattened.

I realised that we were being given the old carrot-and-stick treatment; the carrot was our vested interest in delaying the right-fighter development, and the stick was the threat of successive sorties against alerted defences. I didn't realise how cynical the treatment was until much later, when we learned that Peenemunde was the development site for the enemy's new V-weapons. This clumsy encouragement, whoever decided to offer it, seemed to me misguided and distasteful.

Halifaxes and Stirlings were to open the attack by bombing the scientists' living quarters. Lancasters of 5 Group were to hit the airfield, and we I Group squadrons were to aim at the factories. A small force of

Mosquitoes was to attack Berlin, in an attempt to draw the night-fighters away from us.

We got DV222 George Two off the ground at twenty-three minutes to ten and, washed in the unaccustomed moonlight, set course east. Tail winds brought us early to our check-point in the Baltic, and I throttled back to lose time as we came to Rügen Island, north-west of the target. Peenemunde lay starkly lighted by the moon, marked by green TIs, while a master-bomber circled, marshalling the attack. At thirty-four minutes after midnight I set George Two's nose at the target on a time and distance run, and Larry dropped the bombs from 9,000 feet; a 4,000 pounder, six 1,000 pounders, and two 500 pounders. A billowing smoke screen partially obscured the target, but did not deter his aim. We swung right on to 290° true, against a forty-knot headwind, and climbed hard.

We had reached 18,000 feet near Stralsund, when the first fighter appeared, and the longest ten minutes I had known began. The "boozer" light, flashing on my panel, gave the first warning that we were being followed, and then Lanham picked him up from the rear turret.

"Fighter, fighter. Stand by to cork-screw port."

"Standing by."

"Mid-upper from rear-gunner. He's at seven o'clock low. There may be a pair. I'll look after this one, you watch out for the other."

"Okay, Charlie."

"Prepare to cork-screw port . . . cork-screw port . . . go."

"Going port."

I rolled George Two sharply left, and dropped the nose. I let her go through ten degrees before pulling to the right and up, levelled as she passed back through the homeward heading, dived through another ten degrees right, then climbed her back to port through twenty degrees. Charlie kept the patter going, giving me the fighter's distance and position, then:

"Foxed him, Jack. He's holding off on the starboard quarter. Now he's going low astern. He's out of range. Stand by."

George Protheroe, slowly rotating the mid-upper turret, pressed his microphone switch.

"Another fighter, skipper, four o'clock high, six hundred yards. It's an Me210."

Charlie broke in.

"Watch him, George. Here comes number one. Corkscrew starboard . . . go."

"Going starboard."

Between us, the gunners and I evaded four attacks. There were eleven degrees of frost at our height, but, after throwing George Two about the sky for a few minutes, I was sweating like a horse, and my muscles were aching. While one fighter attacked, the other held off, content to retain one gunner's attention. They were never in Lanham's field of fire, and the mid-upper guns stayed silent. A feeling of despair began to crawl into my mind; inevitably I would become exhausted and the fighters' shells would rip George Two to shreds. They could afford to take their time. Perhaps the sadistic bastards were just playing with us. I pressed my back against the armour-plate behind me, and wondered what protection it would give. Come on then, Messerschmitt, I thought, get it over with.

Turning automatically into another cork-screw to the left, I looked over my shoulder, down the length of the port wing. There he was, less than a hundred yards away, and converging, trying to bring his guns to bear. I saw a helmeted head in the cockpit, and a surge of anger pushed my lethargy away. I stared at the German pilot. You're no good, I thought. You re a damned poor shot and a bloody awful pilot. Why the hell doesn't the mid-upper fire? I snapped the mike switch on.

"For Christ's sake, George, shoot that bastard down!"

At once, the guns chattered, and a stream of orange sparks curved slowly down and through the fighter's nose. He rolled over on his back, and dived straight down, disappearing into a sheet of stratus thousands of feet below.

"I think you got him. Where's the other one?"

Lanham answered from the rear turret.

"Falling back astern. He's clearing off. Good shooting, George!"

I agreed.

"Yes, well done, George! What kept you?"

"Sorry, skipper. I had my sights on him all the time. I think I just forgot to shoot."

I sat relaxed and let the relief run over me. George Two sailed on securely in the cold and moonlit night. I thought about the little Welsh mid-upper gunner, barely eighteen years old, rigid in his turret through the combat, unable to press the triggers until he heard my angry shout.

The Peenemunde raid, on which nearly 600 bombers were deployed, and forty lost, including the "A" Flight Commander from Wickenby, was perhaps the most important on which we were engaged. We later learned that it delayed the enemy's V-bomb attacks on England by six crucial months.

There had been no heavy bomber attack on Berlin since March. I didn't think we would be sent there until the nights grew longer, but I was wrong. We crowded into the briefing room on Monday, 23 August, and stared at the ribbon on the map.

"Cripes, it's the big city."

"What did I tell you?"

"You said Nürnberg."

"I said Nürnberg or Berlin. I knew it when they put 18,50 gallons in the tanks. I thought it'd be Berlin."

We took old Charlie Two, a Mark I Lancaster W4370, and we had a cookie, three 1000 pounders, and the incendiaries on board. I climbed for fifty minutes over base, and set course for Mablethorpe at twenty past nine. We crossed the Dutch coast near Alkmaar at quarter past ten, and flew on to the east, passing south of Bremen, across Lüneburg Heath, the Altmark plains and Brandenburg. At midnight we were thirty miles south-east of the German capital. There we turned north-westward to attack, and, ignoring a dummy city on our track, pointed Charlie Two's nose at the markers which were lighting up the city's heart.

Charlie Two sailed smoothly in between the questing searchlight fingers, but a shell burst underneath us made her rattle like a side-drum as the fragments beat her skin. Over other targets, flak and searchlights in alliance had been the chief defence; fighters had eschewed the target area and been content to harass us *en route*. Berlin's defence was of a different order: flak was secondary, and the sky was full of fighters, looking for us with the searchlights' help.

We briefly witnessed many combats; a bomber tilting in the cone of lights, then the slowly-curving streams of tracer, the lights going off to find another target, the fighter hunting do in his blinded prey. To watch the bakes to the end was tempting, but the secret of survival was to keep a roving eye. I saw one bomber's silhouette against the glowing city — it fell in a shallow dive, the port wing streaming flame.

"Pilot to navigator. Lancaster going down on the port bow, port wing on fire. Will you log it?"

"Okay."

"There's a parachute just opened. Count how many get out if you can, Larry."

High on the starboard beam another combat flickered, reciprocating bursts of gunfire out of nowhere into blackness. The night was full of sudden lights, and I dropped my seat down to its lowest setting, so that the cockpit shielded me better from the distraction of the scene. Larry's words came Like a blessing.

"Bombs gone. Bomb-doors closed."

I pulled the bomb-door lever, and felt the change of trim as the doors shut out the air flow.

"Doors closed."

"Good run, skip, should be bang on target."

Myring sounded gleeful. I imagined him rubbing his hands together, as he stared down past his bomb-sight at the bursting high explosive in the streets below, anticipating the aiming point photograph that would be displayed outside the briefing room at Wickenby. The name of Myring would be etched upon that photograph, and would be seen by all, a name to reckon with, a credit to his skipper, to his squadron, to Australia. I sometimes thought it was as well that no picture came into his mind of shattered limbs, of burning clothing, of living bodies crushed by rubble. He only saw a coloured target-indicator, as he squinted through his bomb-sight, and thumbed the release button. Maybe I had greater imaginative resources, but at such times they seemed to be switched off. My mind was just as closed as Larry's; as I held the aircraft steady for his aim I saw no bloody pictures, had no memories of what I'd seen in London in the blitz. I pulled my seat up to its normal level, and swung the nose to starboard.

When we had cleared the deep defences of the city, I turned north-north-west towards the Baltic Sea. We left the German coast near Restock, and headed west-north-west to pass south of the Danish islands, and across the mainland north of Flensburg on the frontier, where a storm of flak attacked the sky. Another half hour's flying brought us to the shore of the North Sea, above the Frisian Islands, and we kept well to the north of the threatening guns on Sylt.

Cassidy's task of laying our courses was assisted for the first time on this mission by PFF-laid marker flares, dropped at certain points along the route. The aid was welcomed by the navigator, but there clearly was a danger that it also showed the fighters where to find us. The gunners, therefore, scanned the sky with extra care, and I was glad to leave the telltale yellow flares behind us.

One of the more experienced captains on the squadron, Ashburner, was among the fifty-seven who failed to return from this operation, on which 719 aircraft set out. Many aerial combats were reported by those who did return, and we knew that the enemy now had over five hundred radar-equipped night-fighters to deploy against us. No doubt about it, Berlin was a tough target, and I had an idea that we were going to see a lot more of it before we finished.

Four nights later, on 27 August, we flew DV200 Fox Two to Nürnberg. Our target was the north-west quarter of the city, where, we were coolly told at briefing, the density of population was the highest in all Germany. We traversed London's dockland on the way to Beachy Head, crossing into France at le Tréport. Then on, past spiteful Amiens, past Luxembourg and south of Mannheim and eastward into Bavaria. There was no cloud, and the visibility was good, as we turned on 330° magnetic to drop the bombs from 21,000 feet. Myring had a green target-indicator in his bomb-sight at thirteen minutes to one, paused one second to compensate for the accustomed tendency to creep-back, and pressed the button. He briefly commented:

"Lot of good fires going — well concentrated, too, I'd say."

We plodded back to Wickenby to land at half past four. Another aircrew was missing, that of Warrant Officer Aspden. Later we were told that the attack had fallen east of the aiming point, among the temporary homes of refugees from bombed Berlin. This dubious intelligence was imparted with sardonic humour, and raised a hollow, sycophantic laugh, as though our inaccuracy might be excused by this fortuitous calamity.

A new flight commander introduced morning parades for the aircrew. We took the first of these as something of a joke, but it turned out that the new man was quite serious about it. He marched slowly along our ranks, with McLaughlin and a warrant officer uncomfortably in tow, and inspected each of us. He found much to criticise. It was true that we had grown rather lax; we wore the most comfortable clothes that came to hand, and we didn't always shave in the morning. Saluting was generally avoided. Several Australians wore slouch hats, and a Canadian gunner affected a yellow Stetson. Most of us wore one or two items of flying-gear. I was dressed in a US Army shirt, silk scarf, sweater, basketball boots, and battledress with no cap. The Flight Commander eyed me narrowly.

"What are you supposed to be?"

"Sir?"

"What are you?"

"Sergeant Pilot Currie, sir."

"In what service?"

I giggled nervously. The Flight Commander frowned. "Stand still and answer my question."

"The Air Force, sir."

"Which air force?"

"Ours, sir. The Royal Air Force."

"I've seen smarter men in an Egyptian sanitary squad. You've got half an hour to get properly dressed and report back to my office. Dismiss."

It wasn't easy. I had to ransack the rest of the crew's kit bags to get a full uniform together.

Our new Flight Commander might have transformed us into a reasonably smart unit in time, but he went missing after a few trips, and we reverted to normal.

The food in the Sergeants' Mess was nothing to shout about, and the most acceptable meal was the bacon and eggs that we customarily received before a mission. It was beneficial to have the Australians in the crew, because they were sent food parcels from home: tinned chicken, condensed milk, chocolate, and tinned cheese. In flight, we had orange juice, chocolate bars and chewing-gum. We were also provided with meat or fish-paste sandwiches, but they were always curled up at the edges by the time we were hungry enough to eat them, so we used to give them to the ground-crew boys before take-off.

I was always acutely conscious of the rhythm of the engines, and it worried me if they were not in perfect synchronisation. Johnny Walker tried to set the pitch levers so that the propellers turned at the same rpm, and then I fiddled with them until the sound was exactly right, like the beat of a single pulse. If there was any sort of light, it was easier to synchronise them by adjusting the pitch until the shadows on each pair of propellers were at the same angle. Even when we thought we had got them right, one engine would eventually wander off into a rhythm of its own, and any change of pitch for tactical reasons — climb, descent, evasive action — would mean starting all over again. On the way home from a long-range sortie, I fell into a doze on rare occasions but invariably awoke sitting bolt upright, cold with fear, hand on the throttles, eyes on the gauges, because my sleeping brain was failing to register the sound of the engines, and the reflex thought process told me that they had stopped. The shock would then keep me awake for a while, but, once somnolence had set in, it would overtake me again before long. The answer to that was to take a caffeine tablet, and hope the effect would wear off before getting home to base and bed.

Some cynic had said that flying a heavy bomber meant hours of acute boredom with occasional moments of blind panic. There was enough truth in the remark to raise a smile of recognition, but, like most aphorisms, it didn't really fill the bill. There were times when man, machine and nature came together in a harmony that was the height of happiness. These moments could occur quite normally, on any routine flight from A to B, but they never failed to thrill me to the heart. Take an ordinary weather situation, in which an area of low pressure is centred over Scotland. Somewhere around Edinburgh is the apex of a triangle, the base of which runs along the English Channel. The right side of the triangle, lying from Scotland to the Frisian Islands, is a warm front, thick with cloud and full of rain. The left side is the following cold front, dropping showers from towering cumulus along the western hills of Britain. Within the triangle is the warm sector, which pokes a moist tongue of air between the colder atmospheric masses on either side. Late in the afternoon, the sky over Lincolnshire is a grey overcast. Beneath the slowly moving blanket, the visibility is poor, and there is a tendency to drizzle where nimbo-stratus is mixed in with the strato-cumulus.

The laden Lancaster runs along the wetly gleaming runway, and launches itself into the miasma. The fields below are grey and ghostly as you set the climbing power and edge the nose round on to course. The world disappears. Blindness creeps in through the cockpit windows, colourless and enervating. Your rate of climb is better than that of a one-legged drunk trying to walk up a down-coming escalator, but not much. The engines echo dully in your ears as you try to hold the air speed steady and the course on 090°. You remember all those unseen Lancasters around you, and wonder if it wouldn't be a good idea to wear your parachute. The aircraft crawls upward like a heliotrope inching through the soil towards the sun. After what seems like many hours of this (the Omega on your wrist has obviously stopped), you notice that the gloom is fractionally lightening. Somewhere up there is daylight, for the reaching. Of course, it could be just a shallow corridor of open sky, with further layers of cloud above it. Wait and see. It's definitely getting lighter. And suddenly the cockpit of the Lancaster breasts the cloud tops, and there is the sky, vast and clear and brilliantly blue. The wisps of cloud that rush past you are so white that you can't believe you've ever seen true whiteness before. It's whiter than babies' teeth and angels' wings. High above, there are some scattered streaks of cirrus, underlining the splendour of the sun, and as for those six hundred bombers, you can see less than a dozen, at different heights and tiny in the distance. There's really plenty of room for everybody.

If there were time to spare for fun, it would be good to hold this height for a while and run along the cloud crests, like surf-riding on a sea of cotton wool. It's one of the very few times in flight that you can get any real impression of speed. But you need all the time you've got to climb this aeroplane to 20,000 feet, so you go on up, marvelling at the scene that gradually spreads out below. That great expanse of clouds, which made a dirty ceiling for the earth, has now become a pure white floor for heaven, as far as the eye can see. It is a tranquil scene, of transcendent beauty.

Forget the fact that the gradually decreasing atmospheric pressure is making you want to fart, close your ears to the rumble of the engines, ignore the mass of machinery and dials around you, and don't look at the lantern jaw of the flight engineer, steadily chewing gum beside you. This experience is something of a translation, in the biblical sense of conveyance to heaven without death.

There was another sort of situation that I found breathtakingly beautiful, and it occurred in the same meteorological conditions. The warm front lay between us and the target, and the low cloud of the warm sector hid the coastline when we set course east from Mablethorpe. Fifty miles out over the North Sea, the light was fading quickly, but I could nevertheless discern a massive build-up far ahead. We climbed on slowly, much more slowly than the cloud tops rose to meet us, as layer grew on layer until they merged to make a wall of cloud. Three miles below us, the nimbo-stratus poured steady rain into the sea; around us, the alto-stratus mixed with alto-cumulus; above, cirrus and cirro-stratus blotted out the sky. By the time we crossed the coast of Holland, at 18,000 feet, we were in total darkness and deep inside the frontal mass. And so we travelled for an hour or so, blindly into Germany, while Cassidy mapped our position by dead reckoning, Myring warmed himself with thoughts of beer and Melbourne's sunshine, Walker chewed gum and watched the gauges, Fairbairn listened patiently to static on his headphones, and the gunners swung their sightless turrets to and fro.

Characteristically, the front has sent its topmost cloud far in advance of the main mass, and from that high leading cirrus, just below the tropopause, the profile of the front is angled back towards the lower levels like an overhanging shelf. Most times, the discontinuity was not well marked; the division between cold air and warm was blurred, and we would emerge gradually into clearer skies, with other cloud around us at various distances and heights. But on this occasion, we burst out of the cloud into an open sky, and the whole expanse of Lüneburg Heath spread 20,000 feet below. As the last time we had seen the ground was over Lincolnshire three hours before, the effect was startling. I felt as though I had woken in the middle of the night, and opened my eyes to find that my bedstead and I had been lifted into outer space while I was sleeping.

It was a moment of some unreality. I rocked the wings gently to reassure my senses, and had a good look around. Behind us, there was nothing to be seen but the steeply leaning wall of the warm front. Below, a river snaked across the darkly wooded plain, showing its course in places by reflections of the sublight. Above, the frontal cirrus made a screen to hide the stars. Ahead of us, although the line between dark sky and darker earth was almost imperceptible, the suggestion of a horizon was just enough to use for reference. The Lancaster throbbed powerfully, her engines sounding like a quartet of Stentors in unison, but there was no other aircraft, nor any other living thing, within my sight. I had the illusion that we had emerged into a world at peace. All was still, save us. All slept, save us. Perhaps the war was over; Hitler was dead, by act of man or God. Germany had surrendered while we were in the air, the raid had been recalled, we hadn't heard the signal. Alone, we would fly on to drop our bombs on an undefended target.

I wriggled on my seat cushion, and tried to concentrate my thoughts on rationality. Then, a long way to the north, I saw a handful of searchlights waving their pallid fingers at the night. The fantasy was over. I called the navigator:

"We're through the front, Jim. I can see searchlights on the port beam. Might be thirty, forty miles away."

"Oh, good on yer, Jack. That ought to be Hamburg. We're not too bad for time, if it is."

You weren't supposed to smoke in the aeroplane, but on the long ride home over the North Sea the temptation was usually too strong for me. When we had descended below oxygen height, I would ask the flight engineer if he could smell petrol. He would pull his mask off, and sniff round the cockpit like an excited dog. When he had announced that he could smell nothing, the bomb-aimer would light two cigarettes and pass one back for me. Walker fell for it every time.

"Hey, I thought you said you could smell petrol!"

"No, I asked you if you could."

Then I would loosen my straps, engage the automatic pilot, sit back and really enjoy that cigarette. At those moments, cruising home on half power with the darkness, while the dawn began to touch the sky behind my left shoulder with a few bright strokes of gold, the crew cocooned in warm leather and fur, lulled by the gently throbbing metal, the terrors of the night would soon disperse. A few hundred miles ahead lay the coast of England, beyond it the Lincolnshire fields, breakfast and bed. The next briefing seemed a long way off.

Between the passing night and the emerging day the bomber floated, steady and secure. I could, if I wished, for a time postpone the dawn: push down the nose, lose enough height to mask the daylight with the eastern horizon, and it would still be yesterday.

Unlike the enemy coastal searchlights, groping and gathering, clutching and clinging, the beam at Mablethorpe stood steady and alone, eight or nine minutes flying time from base. Then the girl's voice from the watch office gave the landing drill, the height to join the circuit. You dropped down through the stack of homing aircraft in your turn, heard the slipstream change as the main wheels thrust from their housing, felt the surge as the landing power came on, and sensed the change of trim as the flaps bent down. The Lancaster swung towards the runway lights, crabbed down the approach, and swept across the threshold. The throttled engines coughed, the rudders twitched the nose straight down the runway's centre-line, the wheels flirted with the concrete, kissed, withdrew, and finally embraced.

At debriefing there was a mug of cocoa and a tot of rum for each of the crew, dispensed by the padre. Only Myring liked the rum, so we gave him the other six tots, and he sang all the way back to the hut.

I don't know what slight sound or movement woke me in the night-dark Nissen hut. I listened to the unconscious breathing of the crew. As my vision cleared, I realised from the shielded glow that the eccentric Myring was reading by the glimmer of a flashlight. I lay still and suddenly felt the flesh above my neck begin to creep. In my sleep I had pulled a pillow from under my head, and it lay on the bed beside me. Sitting in the middle of that pillow, a lean brown rat methodically groomed its paws.

I continued to lie still, but my stillness was that of a rigor. My voice came out between a whisper and a squeak.

"Christ, it's a rat!"

Larry stirred under his blankets.

"Hang on, skip. I'll fix the bastard."

I nearly went cross-eyed trying to watch the rat and Larry without moving my head. His flashlight swept towards me, and I saw the gleam of a revolver barrel beside it. I was out of the bed and flat on the floor faster than the speed of thought. Bedclothes, pillows and rat went flying. Larry sat up and shook his head reprovingly.

"Aw, gee, Jack. You shoulda laid still. I'da picked the bastard off with one shot."

I stumbled to my feet, shivering.

"You crazy sod. Put that bloody gun away."

We peered about for the rat, muttering at each other, but it had disappeared. Johnny's muffled voice whined in a corner.

"Shut up, can't you? Some of us are trying to get some sleep."

If our quarters were liable to be visited by rodents, so were our aeroplanes prone to occasional infestation, not by mice or rats, but by the troublesome spirits known as gremlins. They blocked oxygen tubes, and pulled out intercom plugs. There was a gremlin whose pleasure it was to put the auto-pilot out of action when you had a three-hour leg to fly across the sea, and another who liked to wedge himself inside the pitot-tube, so that you couldn't read the airspeed. One particularly naughty, and fortunately rare, gremlin saved himself for the end of a trip. Then he either fixed it so that one of the wheels wouldn't lock down, or made you think it wasn't locked by putting a green light out of action. Better still, he would keep a few bombs on board by holding the release gear shut when the bomb-aimer pressed the button. That added interest to the landing.

Taking off could also have complications. On an ideal aircraft, you would simply open the throttles "smoothly and firmly", as the instructors used to say, and off you would go, accelerating steadily, right down the runway centre-line. Unfortunately, nature and a few odd laws of physics combined to ensure that nothing as simple as that happened. For one thing, the wind rarely blew straight down the runway, and any crosswind element pressed against the upwind side of the fuselage and tried to turn the aeroplane that way. The other factors, which I but dimly understood, resulted from the way the propellers turned. First, an airscrew spinning round is subject to the same forces as affect a gyroscope, and one of these converts a push at any point on the gyro's plane into a turning motion, not, as you might think, in the direction of the pressure, but at right angles to it. So when you pushed the stick forward in the Lancaster to get the tail off the ground, you were also giving the airscrews all the excuse they needed to exercise a smart left turn, taking the aircraft with them. Next, the slipstream from the props didn't flow back down the fuselage evenly, but twisted round it like a cork-screw, pushing the aircraft out of line. Last, there was a force which instructors used to introduce by saying "I am now going to talk about torque", and then write the word on the blackboard so that you got the point of the joke. I got the impression that torque made the aircraft try to turn around the prop-shafts, instead of sitting still and letting the props get on with their job. Anyway the effect was that more weight was put on one wheel than the other, thus acting like a brake on that side.

The result of all this was that, even in zero wind, the Lanc on take-off wanted to go left, and if the wind was coming more from that direction, you had to be ready to correct it with the rudders and the engines. One of our pilots failed to do this, going off fully laden for the Ruhr one night. He started a nasty swing to port quite early in his run, couldn't check it and went on to the grass. That was the point of decision. He could either cut everything and try to stop before he ran out of airfield, or he could keep going in the hope that he could get back on the runway without hitting anything on the way. He chose the second alternative, and the Lancaster hurtled across the airfield like a juggernaut, at an angle of 45° to the runway, bumping and bouncing, engines screaming at emergency power.

A ground-crew flight sergeant, cycling along the perimeter track on his way back from a far-away dispersal, was neatly decapitated by a prop-blade of the port outer engine. Oblivious of this misfortune, the crew wiped their brows as their bomber staggered into the air, and went on their eastward way. Next day, news of the headless NCO was passed to the pilot, and he took it badly. The incident seemed to shatter his already shaken confidence, and he could be observed, white-faced and hollow-eyed, standing alone in the mess or crew room for several days, before disappearing from the squadron scene.

This was a tragic and unusual departure, which was recorded with as little passion as were postings of a routine nature. The official records also showed our casualties and their replacements, absences on leave or temporary duty, and the occasional promotions. The latter were not liberally awarded; our first tour gunners, engineers and wireless-ops seldom rose above the rank of sergeant, although their comrades from the Commonwealth fared better. Pilots and navigators, if they began their tours as sergeants, might expect one or two advancements, some through flight sergeant to warrant rank, others direct to pilot officer.

My commissioning board consisted of one visiting Squadron Leader. He borrowed an office in the squadron headquarters, and we candidates queued outside. I had been before a full-scale board a year before in America, and had at that time asked to be excused, giving the grounds that I thought I was too young to hold commissioned rank. The real reason was that I longed to get back to England, and most of the cadets who were commissioned in the States stayed there as instructors. I was homesick, and I wanted to become an operational pilot.

Now, I was glad of another chance, although I was pleased to have been a sergeant pilot. It is unlikely that I should have got to know the crew so well if I had been an officer from the start.

My relationship with Jimmy Cassidy certainly hadn't suffered from the fact that he held a commission and I did not. I was pleased for his sake that he was an officer, although there were times when it was a nuisance to have him living in a different mess. From the beginning we called each other by Christian names, although, strictly speaking, the rest of us should have called him "Sir". That would really have embarrassed him. Sergeant Lanham sometimes addressed the bomb-aimer as "Flight Sergeant", not for reasons of protocol, but to imply a mocking disapproval of Myring's seniority.

The rank structure among bomber-crews was pretty peculiar, with many captains holding sergeant's rank. I only knew of one crew of which the pilot was not the captain, and that was not because a member of his crew out-ranked him but because he didn't fit the captain's role. He was thought to be too ready to accept suggestions from his crew that it would be a good idea to abandon a sortie for reasons of some minor snag, so the commissioned navigator was made captain, and the crew made some improvement in their record of missions carried out. But it must have been a tricky situation, as the navigator would be in no position to make any of the immediate tactical decisions that came a pilot's way.

The commissioning interview was painless, and lasted less than five minutes.

I never met our Commander-in-Chief, never saw him, never heard his voice. Although the aircrews referred to him familiarly as Butch Harris, he was in fact distanced from us by such far echelons of rank and station, that he was a figure more of imagination than reality. Uninhibited by any bounds of truth, we were able to ascribe to him any characteristic that our spirits needed. It pleased us to think of him as utterly callous, indifferent to suffering, and unconcerned about our fate. There was a paradoxical comfort in serving such a dread commander: no grievance, no complaint, no criticism could possibly affect him. You might as well complain to Jupiter that the rain was wet.

We chose to believe that Harris lived in utter luxury at Claridges, and that with his morning beverage a servant brought him a jewelled dart, which he casually cast at a wall map of Europe above his dressing-table. He would then take up the silver scrambler telephone, and call High Wycombe.

"This is the Commander-in-Chief. The target for tonight is . . ."

Once it seemed that we might see him. He was to deliver an address at Binbrook, a dozen miles to our north-east, and mine was one of the Wickenby crews detailed to attend. We packed into an airfield truck, as uncomfortably as any parcel of pilgrims on the desert road to Mecca, and set off. Inevitably, the truck broke down five miles out of Wickenby, and the face of Harris remained hidden from our gaze.

In August the Flight Commander gave me a copy of an official paper which bore the heading: "Command Routine Orders by Air Chief Marshal Sir Arthur Harris, KCB, OBE, AFC".

It commended my action on the Hamburg raid in glowing terms. I looked anxiously at the foot of the page — it would have been inconsistent with my image of Harris if he had signed so fulsome a piece. All was well. The signature was that of a subordinate officer.

I showed the order to my crew; they were unexcited.

"What are you gonna do with that?"

"I don't know. Stick it in my log-book, I suppose."

"Yeah, well, you can't pin it on your chest, can you? Look, Flying Officer Wossname gets bounced on Hanover because he can't fly right, and half his crew shot up — immediate bloody DFC. You bring us back safe and sound, 'cept for a bump on Johnny's nut — and get bugger-all. A piece of paper!"

"Oh, well. Most gongs are all balls, anyway. You've usually got to have bought it before you get the best ones."

I had been surprised at the time, when people said I was sure to get a medal, because the return of Baker Two seemed to me to be a simple case of self-preservation. Some six months later, the award of DFCs to Cassidy, Lanham and me, and of a DFM to Fairbairn, was promulgated. In due course, I received the medal through the post, with a letter from King

George VI, regretting that he was unable to give it to me personally. I could understand that, and would have settled for having it pinned on by the dread Harris, but it seemed he had no dispensation to perform that service for His Majesty.

I suppose the nearest we came to contact with the Commander-in-Chief was when a message from him was read to us at briefing on 8 July. It simply told us:

"You are to complete the destruction of the old city of Cologne."

That kindled a glow of recognition, and an awe of measureless authority.

On 30 August, my mother wrote, ". . . we heard them going out last Friday, and I went outside and looked up and wondered if you were up there — it was too dark to see anything but stars. I am so thankful you are safe, darling. I pray so hard every night that you may be kept safe and given wisdom and courage. We are very delighted to read what you say about your crew; personally, I am quite sure they are the finest crew in the RAF . . ."

CHAPTER
FIVE

Fifteen Gone,
Fifteen to Go

As August ended, squadron commanders came and went like rain in spring. I was surprised when Woody left; I had thought him timeless and invulnerable, part of the establishment. A girl in Flying Control told me that Woody was watching from the tower when I took off in Easy Two for the crew's first operational flight — the gardening run to La Rochelle. Two more new captains took off that night, he watched them go in silence. But of me he said:

"She's going to be all right."

Sure enough, of those three crews, only mine survived the tour. His own tour now complete, he left with suitable distinction and acclaim, to be the chief instructor at a training field. His successor in command was lost without delay, flying with an inexperienced crew. His name appeared in orders, and was gone. I never saw his face.

This brief incumbency brought on a pause, before the training machine produced a new commander for

the squadron. Meanwhile, the senior Flight Commander filled the hole. At length, the new man came, in
well-cut uniform and polished buttons, with healthy,
unlined cheeks and eyes unshadowed. As we weighed
him up, and watched his first attempts at bomber
missions, I knew that we had suffered a great loss. The
squadron now would never be the same. While the
veteran Wood was there, I had been able to ignore the
vanishing Lancasters and crews. He was there before an
op. and after, I had linked my continuity with his. Now
the totem stood no longer, the new men failed or
fumbled, they held command through circumstance of
rank.

The Station Commander did his best. He flew
himself with untried crews, took the briefings, spoke
with knowledge. But he was of the station, not the
squadron. He did not have to fly, his destiny was
different from ours. Wood was gone, and veteran crews
were missing — mortality was evident throughout. The
squadron after all was just a number, and its
commanders had no permanence. If, as it seemed, their
ability was less or their luck worse than mine, the more
must my faith be pinned on the Lancaster and on the
crew.

I decided that I needed some promotion. I had been
a sergeant pilot for a year, and had heard no more of
my commission (it came through later, back-dated to
July). Meanwhile my navigator was promoted to the
rank of Flying Officer, and my bomb-aimer, the
ineffable Larry, became a Warrant Officer, moustaches
bristling. What of me, their captain? I became a flight

sergeant by auto-promotion; I bought brass crowns, and sewed them on my sleeves above the tapes. No one noticed, no one cared. I was still sergeant in the battle order, and my pay did not improve, but I felt better.

We were briefed for Berlin again on Tuesday 31 August, but our aircraft wouldn't start. We clambered out, cursing in the twilight, carrying the parachutes, the helmets, the rations and the life-jackets, and transferred to the reserve aircraft. Sweating from the effort in the heavy flying-kit, we climbed aboard and began another starting sequence. This time, an oil-leak stopped us. Again we disembarked, unloaded, and trudged back to the first aircraft. The other Lancasters rolled by to take-off, the ground crews laboured, the vans and motor-cycles of the engineers buzzed across the airfield to the invalid bomber.

The squadron aircraft climbed above us, roaring harshly as the Merlins pulled them higher in the clouded, darkening sky. We waited, squatting on our parachutes, chewing our gum and staring at the scene. I borrowed a cigarette from Larry, and walked away behind the flight hut. I undid straps and tapes and buttons to piddle on the concrete, and saw that an airman had planted a species of daisy in a stone-edged row beside the cinder-path. The straining engines' sound above made me feel desolate and ill-humoured. We'd done the air test in the morning, nurtured the equipment, been to briefing, and eaten the flying-meal. I had made my pre-op motion, got dressed up, and stiffened all the sinews. We'd dragged the kit out to dispersal, and made the pre-flight checks. My mind was prepared to undertake the mission; the waiting-time was nearly over, and now we had no aeroplane to fly.

I rejoined the gloomy circle of my crew; we sat in silence. I looked at my service-issue Omega; it was too late now, even if they got the trouble fixed. We wouldn't be allowed to take off if we couldn't get to the target on time. So be it; probably it was best to leave it to that destiny which shapes our ends. This might have been the one we didn't come back from. I stood up, and Jimmy closed his canvas navigation bag.

"It's past the deadline."

"We've been off after the deadline before now."

"Yeah, but they haven't got it mended yet. I reckon we're scrubbed."

Lanham looked up at the throbbing sky, waved his gauntleted hand, and spoke with an exaggerated English accent:

"Good luck, chaps. Wish I were coming with you."

A crew bus turned into the dispersal, and came to a halt beside us. George Protheroe picked up the navigator's sextant, and opened the rear door of the bus. As I climbed into the front seat beside the driver, I heard Lanham say:

"What d'you say we get a taxi into Lincoln?"

The barmaid in the Saracen's Head gave us a sparkling smile:

"Are you not away to Berlin with the others, then?"

"Not tonight. What makes you think it's Berlin, blondie?"

"Oh, a little bird whispered."

"What little bird?"

"Ah, now, that'd be telling. What can I get you, boys?"

"Four pints of bitter and a shandy. You ought to watch it, blondie — careless talk and all that."

"Only half pints, I'm sorry."

On 30 August the squadron lost another crew, on a trip to München-Gladbach, and Sergeant Green's aircraft was hit by cannon fire from a night-fighter. Next night, Green failed to come back from the Berlin mission, and so did Machin.

On Friday 3 September, the target was Berlin again, for the third time in twelve days. We took a Mark I Lancaster ED392 Dog Two, which was powered by Merlin 22 engines, whereas the Mark III had Merlin 28s. Three hundred Lancasters made the attack, flying in one concentrated wave. As we approached the target, the PFF marker flares began to blossom on the ground. On the radio, the circling master bomber passed instructions to the attackers. On the whole, his words were cool and helpful, but he fell from grace with one slightly patronising remark, which invited a harsh response, and got it.

"Come on in, main force, the searchlights won't bite you!"

Few were the transmit buttons left unpressed, few were the bomber captains who did not reply:

"F . . . off!"

Our bombs went down at twenty-three minutes past eleven, and hit the aiming-point direct, as the flare-lit photograph later showed. After a cloud-enveloped route, the Berlin sky was clear. The night-fighters prowled among the searchlights, and we picked our way out of the defences with anxiety and care.

The stout, and stouter-hearted BBC reporter who recorded his impressions of the scene from a Lancaster cabin selected a good mission for his broadcast, as it turned out to be the most successful of the summer attacks on the big city.

We flew north across the Baltic into Sweden where neutrality was observed by token gunfire, then up the Kattegat and west down the Skagerrak, with the Norwegian coast sliding by on our starboard side. It took Dog Two eight and a half hours to make the sortie, from which two of the most experienced crews at Wickenby failed to return. In all the Command lost twenty-two aircraft out of 320 to set out, of which 295 attacked Berlin.

Among the natural and unnatural phenomena that revealed themselves to us in flight, that which appeared the most unreal was an aurora borealis, which filled the northern sky as we travelled across Sweden. I had seen that luminous radiation once before, standing at the window of a barrack block in Canada, and had admired it as one might a double rainbow or a tropic sunrise. Then it seemed beautiful, and coldly distant. But now, the lights were nearer, shimmering and shaking as if in icy fury. I felt I might reach out and touch them, and be burned, as ice can burn you.

We went to Mannheim again on Sunday 5 September, flying DV190 Baker Two, now recovered from the injuries that I had caused her over Hamburg.

We followed a more southerly route than that we took on 9 August, crossing the French coast near St Valery and passing south of Luxembourg, instead of going north. We flew in cloud for several hours, but emerged into clear skies over the target area, where the massive Mannheim searchlight belt took a wearisome time to penetrate. Warrant Officer Smith from Wickenby was held fast in a searchlight cone for four minutes, and must have been in luck to make his escape. Leader-Williams in Charlie Two was not so fortunate, and he did not return. We were told the next day that the bombing had been accurate.

The following night we went to Munich, taking off at two minutes to eight in Fox Two for the eight-and-a-half-hour trip. The bomber stream flew across Hyde Park *en route* for Beachy Head, to give the London people a rare sight of our numbers. We headed south of east for Freiburg, turning eastward as we crossed the Rhine. Lake Constance gleamed to starboard and, on its northern banks, the guns of Friedrichshaven challenged us with brilliant rainbow showers of flak and flares. I called the navigator:

"Jimmy, come and have a look at this. It's quite a sight."

Cassidy emerged from his curtained desk space, and peered out through the perspex canopy.

"Where is it?"

"Down there, you clot, just in front of the starboard wing."

"Can't see a thing."

It took him several minutes to descry the spectacle, which to the rest of us, with eyes accustomed to the darkness, was dazzling.

Munich's defences were widespread, and fighter flares hung glaring overhead. On our port beam, flame spurted from a slowly falling Halifax, and, like a scavenger, a Junkers 88 prowled and pecked about the dying bomber. Below, the bombing pattern showed a lack of concentration — more widely scattered than that of recent raids. As Larry Myring pressed the bomb-release button, squinting obliquely through the bombsight, Fox Two reacted to the loss of weight by jumping skittishly. I turned the trimming-wheel to keep her level, and the airspeed needle showed a few more knots. We flew on ten miles east to clear the city, then turned south-west to make our track for home. We left a trail of bursting shells behind us, which grew closer as the gunners found their range. As Fox Two lurched and rattled, Lanham barked a warning from his threatened turret seat. I pushed the nose down, headed southward, and we fled away from danger.

Hutchinson ditched his aircraft in the North Sea, and his bomb-aimer and rear-gunner were never seen again; he thought they must still have been in the aircraft when it sank. The five survivors were picked up late next afternoon by the Grimsby Air-Sea Rescue service, and returned to Wickenby.

After the Munich mission, bad weather caused the cancellation of an operation on 9 September, and then we stood down for a fortnight while the squadron navigators learned to use the latest radar, which was code-named H2S. The Lancasters of "A" and "B" flights had the new aid fitted, but we in "C" flight continued to make do with the G-box.

A DSO was awarded to the missing Squadron Leader Slade, whose place as "A" Flight Commander was filled by Gordon Woollatt, second pilot in the Wellington film called *Target for Tonight*. We had lectures about German prisoner-of-war camps, and how to escape from them. We had lectures about evading capture in the first place. I practised my own escape and evasion techniques by dodging the many PT sessions to which we were subjected and, once forced to undergo one, by escaping from it at the earliest opportunity. Then, the Air Officer Commanding 1 Group paid Wickenby a visit; I avoided him also. Fairbairn disliked PT as much as I did, but he was too conscientious to avoid it deliberately. He asked me:

"If we volunteered for another five ops, do you reckon they'd let us off PT?"

When the squadron started serious flying again, we lost two crews at Mannheim, and nearly lost another over Hanover when Gilman's aircraft was hit in the fuselage by heavy flak which blew the mid-upper gunner to pieces. We next flew on Wednesday 29 September, through cloudless skies to Bochum in the Ruhr area. Our aircraft was a Mark III Lancaster, LM321 Howe Two, with Merlin 38 engines, and we carried a cookie, three 1,000 pounders and the usual assortment of incendiary devices. Myring's uncertain pinpointing, as we flew by Texel on the coast of

Holland, earned him a rare burst of abuse from Cassidy.

"Look, Larry, when we've got perfectly clear skies like this you're at least supposed to give me an accurate pinpoint on the coast crossing. What's the matter with you?"

"Aw, I dunno, Jimmy, it's not that easy. All these little bloody islands look the same."

"Their shapes are entirely different. Aw, you might as well read a book for all the use you are to me."

"How can I read a book in this fight? It's bad enough trying to read the map."

"You're sure you've got a map?"

The normally long suffering navigator may have been moved to anger by the thought of how much better he would have been served by the magic eye of H2S, which showed the coastlines clearly, than by the all-too human eye of Myring, peering bloodshot through the darkness.

There was a dense ground haze over Bochum, made thicker by the smoke of many fires, as we approached on 148° magnetic and bombed at four minutes to nine, from 21,000 feet. Ahead of us we saw a phalanx of searchlights, and a profligate expenditure of heavy barrage flak, but we turned sharply to starboard to escape north-westward into harmless blackness. The flight took four hours and three-quarters, and was almost our shortest mission. Our losses were reported to be high.

Next day, I made the usual entries in my log-book and operations record sheet. The latter read:

Date: 29.9.43   Time: 4.45
AIC: LM321   Progressive
                                  total op hours: 101.55

Captain: Self   Allowed or
Target: Bochum   disallowed: A
Sortie no: 15   Remarks: DCO

As thirty sorties constituted the operation tour,
Bochum marked the half-way point for us. Not that this
achievement held any more than mathematical
significance; it brought no promotion, medals or
emoluments, but, to us, it brought a certain
satisfaction. When we joined the squadron, the odds
against our finishing the tour were about seven to one,
now they had shortened to better than four to one.
These statistics never meant much to me, however.
Except when I was cold and tired and frightened, I
always thought we would survive the tour, and my
initial faith in the bomber and in the crew had been
confirmed. I knew that I could fly and land the
Lancaster in really horrid weather, and I knew that
Cassidy, even with the limited aids at his disposal,
could use them well enough to navigate us there and
back. I also knew, from the evidence of Peenemunde,
that the gunners and I could take on a pair of
night-fighters, in conditions ideally suited to them, and
survive the battle. Was I stepping near the deadly trap
of overconfidence?

Some of the old hands thought that there were two
particularly perilous phases in the tour. One was during
the first half dozen missions before you knew the ropes,

and the other occurred at about the twenty-sortie mark, when a spurious euphoria might lure a crew into contributing by carelessness to their own destruction. We were now midway between these phases; we had passed the first through luck and application, aided by the rear-gunner's experience, and I had no real fear of the second, because I saw no signs of our being lulled by any delusions of indestructibility. True, I may have minimised the threat of the night-fighter, for I was sure that if we saw him first and fought, he would go away to find an easier target, but I didn't need that bogey-man to waken me at night, for I had other dreads. I feared the sudden, all-obliterating flak burst, such as had hit aircraft in the stream beside us. And over Lincolnshire I had seen the tangled, burning metal, and the oily plumes of smoke that followed, when two bombers climbed into each other on a clouded autumn evening. So I dreaded mid-air collision, not only when circling over base in cloud, but later, when converging on a rendezvous or target, our aircraft rocked and trembled, and I wondered whether turbulent air was moving us, or perhaps the slipstream of another bomber, which I might see too late to miss. Such demons often perched on my shoulder, prodding me with chilly fingers, stilling the lullaby of over-confidence.

Two nights after the attack on Bochum, our association with the new Charlie Two (EE133) began when we went to Hagen, in the eastern sector of the Ruhr. The town of Dortmund should have lain to starboard of our inward route, but, by mischance, we found ourselves directly over that well-defended place.

The searchlight crews and gunners gave us their undivided attention; I weaved and dodged in desperate concentration, and Charlie Two shook and rattled as the shells burst close around her. A newly fledged navigator, accompanying Cassidy for his first experience of action, got a lesson on the perils of parting company with the stream. Like the ash trees trying to live on the wind-swept fields at Wickenby, our chances of survival were improved by being in the middle of the group.

The aircraft's skin was pierced by many fragments, but she seemed to have sustained no substantial damage as we cleared the danger area, and headed south for Hagen. Then Lanham called me.

"Rear-gunner to pilot. Hello, pilot, this is the rear-gunner calling."

"Go ahead."

"Hello, 'ello, 'ello. Come on, now, pilot, this is your rear-gunner Charlie Lanham calling you on the intercom."

This was most unlike the gunner's customary terse style of speech and, furthermore, it was strictly against the acknowledged rule by which we eliminated needless chatter. I turned my microphone switch again.

"I repeat — go ahead."

"I'm not going ahead. Matter of fact, I'm going backwards."

"You're talking nonsense. Pull yourself together, Charlie."

"I'm trying to pull my tooth-paste. It's the trouble with the tooth-paste that I'm going ahead to tell you all about it."

"Check your oxygen."

"About the Piccadilly tube the tooth-paste in the turret if you'd listen . . ."

"Shut up, rear-gunner. Switch your mike off and check your oxygen."

". . . and I'm trying to tell you I'm pulling a perambulator, a perambulator, pushing it down Piccadilly . . ."

"Rear-gunner, you must keep quiet until we're through the target. That's an order."

"I'm shutting up a parrot's cage in Piccadilly . . . I can hear my parrot . . . my perambulator . . . you . . ."

Mercifully, he fell unconscious as we approached the target, down the eastern margin of the Ruhr, and the intercom was clear for action. Hagen took a heavy pounding without conspicuous reaction, and the major hazards of the mission were reserved for those who found themselves, as we did, over Dortmund on their way into the target, or who tangled with Cologne's defences on the route away from Hagen, as did others we could see. As soon as we had cleared the latter danger, I took Charlie Two down to 10,000 feet, where the natural consistence of the air eliminated the need for artificial oxygen. The reviving Lanham resumed his discourse on parrots and perambulators, but gradually returned to normal as the oxygen cleared his brain. He remembered nothing of his temporary insensibility, and couldn't understand how he had missed the bombing run on Hagen.

We gave the vicious guns of Amiens a wide berth to the north and crossed the French coast westwards in a headlong dive, which brought protests from the crew about the mounting pressure on their eardrums. We landed at Wickenby ten minutes before midnight, and discovered the neat hole in Lanham's oxygen tube, where a fragment of flak had ruptured it. Snell's aircraft had suffered heavier damage, and required major repairs. Next night, 2 October, we stood down while the squadron attacked Munich with twenty-one aircraft, one of which failed to return.

The stiff head waiter at the Saracen's Head, below the Stonebow in the heart of Lincoln, regarded us with disapproval. He deprecated the presence of sergeants in his dining-room (that officers were with them simply condemned those officers as being unfitted for their rank), and he clearly thought our manners far from couth. We asked if it were true that he spied for Hitler; he did not deign to answer. We produced a bottle of George Gerrard's Canadian whisky, and called for ginger ale and glasses; his face expressed the essence of disgust. The food was mediocre, the service slow, but we enjoyed the height of the ceiling, the glitter of the chandeliers, and the novelty of the occasion. High spirits usually encouraged mischief in us, and when the head waiter brought the bill, I looked at it with simulated horror.

"Thirty-five and six! Oh dear, I'm afraid that's rather more than we expected."

He raised his eyebrows fractionally:

"I think you'll find it's in order . . . sir."

"Oh, I'm sure it is. It's just that we're so awfully broke."

He nodded, drumming his fingers gently on the table. "I see." "Wait a minute, let's see how much we've got. There, I've got one and ninepence. How about you, Charlie?"

The Australian patted his pockets, and shrugged.

"Sorry, Jack, I thought it was on you tonight. I'm flat."

"Never mind. George?"

"Two bob and a wooden nickel."

"That's something. Johnny?"

"Elevenpence-ha'penny and a penny stamp."

Larry's pockets were inside out, the only contents a crumpled handkerchief. Fairbairn said quietly:

"It's my one and nine that you've got."

I smiled foolishly at the waiter.

"I'm afraid we're going to be a bit short."

"Yes, you are."

"I've got a cigarette-lighter, and there's Charlie's fountain pen . . ."

He frowned.

"This is not a pawnbroker's shop."

"No, of course not. Look, how would it be if we took a week's leave, and came and worked in the kitchen, washing-up and peeling spuds and so on?"

"You'd have to see the manager about that . . . sir."

"Okay, bring on the manager."

"I'm afraid the manager is not available at the moment."

A diner at the next table called the waiter.

"Charles, bring me the gentleman's bill. I'll be glad to pay for their dinner. If they don't mind, that is?"

I looked at the others; they were trying to keep their faces straight, but I knew the game was up. I thanked the kindly diner:

"It's very good of you, sir. We were having a joke with the waiter. I think we've got enough, really, thanks all the same."

Protheroe and Myring scolded me later in the bar.

"Why didn't you let him pay, he wanted to, and you could tell he could afford it. That whacking great cigar he was smoking would cost me a week's pay."

"Yeah, gripes, Jack — we coulda gone down the market-place and spent the money on grog."

CHAPTER
SIX

The King's Commission

When I was commissioned, I had to vacate the wooden hut in which I had lived with the rest of the NCOs of the crew since we came to Wickenby, and join Jimmy in the officers' site among the pine trees, on the far side of the domestic area. There was little difference in the accommodation, and I missed the bickering and humour of the crew around me. However, I appreciated the comparative comfort of the officers' mess, less crowded and better furnished than that of the sergeants, and there was some pleasure to be drawn from the rise in pay and status. My salary as a heavy bomber captain, now holding King George VI's commission, was a few pennies over twenty pounds a month. I opened an overdraft with the Westminster Bank, and travelled by the crowded train to London, to equip myself with uniform. I bought the cap, tunic, trousers and greatcoat from Burton's for twenty-five pounds; the raincoat cost three pounds at Burberry's; and Horne's provided the shirts and socks, with some bits and pieces, for twelve pounds, seven shillings and a penny. The pilot's wings I drew from stores for nothing.

The flight commander who was keen about parades would have approved of my appearance, had he lived to see it, but he was succeeded by another, whose interest lay in horticulture. We were provided with the implements to cultivate the barren ground about our huts. Under duress, we applied ourselves spasmodically to gardening when there was no flying, but our lack of enthusiasm was reflected in the negligible results that were achieved.

I preferred to get off camp when we had a stand down, and join others of the crew in working for a farmer down the lane. One of the attractions of the farm was the pretty art-student from London, "holidaying on the land" to drive the tractor, her blonde hair shining in the sunlight; another was the massive farmhouse tea-time spread. The rear-gunner and I shot at rabbits as they scampered from the harvesters, and it was encouraging to find that Lanham sometimes hit one. My own inaccuracy didn't surprise me, as it had already been disappointingly revealed during training in America. There my instructor, the hatchet-faced Lieutenant Seana, had spent despairing hours with me on the clay-pigeon range.

"Just hit one, for Chris' sake, Currie, and we can all go to chow."

We climbed the hill to camp with our wages in the form of eggs carried in the inside pockets of our battledress blouses. One gleaming September afternoon I was kept on duty while Jimmy and the gunners went happily to the farm, grinning, and promising to look after the golden tractor driver. I met the navigator coming back, dirty-faced and cheerful. I embraced him closely, and laughed as I felt the egg-shells breaking under his blouse.

That night Myring and I attended a seance in the big farm kitchen, with McLaughlin, his navigator Tiny Watson and his Canadian mid-upper gunner George Gerrard. The medium was May, the farmer's wife, and she sat tensely with her husband at the heavy, deal table on which we all had placed our hands, palms down. The only light was that which came from the glow of the open kitchen range. There was a smell of whitewash, of apples and, faintly, of manure. May had reported favourably upon the present circumstances of Larry's deceased mother and, more uncertainly, on those of Gerrard's grandfather. Now she was in communication with the spirit of our late flight commander. McLaughlin said:

"Would you ask him, madam, how he came to get the chop?"

The medium relayed the inquiry in her flat, Lincolnshire accent, spacing out the words as though she were speaking to the deaf, rather than the dead.

"Your friends — would like — to know — how — you came — to get — er, shot down. Please answer in the usual way."

She commenced slowly to recite the alphabet, but she had got no further than "B" before the table tilted sharply towards the fireplace. Next time, she progressed as far as "L" before the table rocked again. At length, we had the message "Blasted flak", and I saw McLaughlin's forehead gleam in the firelight as he nodded sagely. The medium's thin shoulders were hunched in an effort of concentration; her hair, escaping the restraint of many pins lay in strands upon her cheeks. Watson's heavy elbow nudged my arm, and his muttered suggestion resonated in the silent kitchen.

"Ask him if he's got any advice to give us."

"Is there — any advice — you wish — to give — your friends?"

Something sharply rapped the table, once, and we knew that this signified an affirmative reply.

"Will you — give us — your — advice?"

Again, the medium intoned the alphabet, and at each selected letter the table tilted on to two legs, and fell back with a thud upon the straw mat lying beneath it. I noticed that Gerrard, who was seated opposite to me, had ducked his head below the tabletop, and was making surreptitious use of a pocket flashlight. As he reappeared the message ended, and May recapitulated triumphantly:

"Stick to navigation!"

Watson's chuckle echoed her satisfaction.

"He's dead right. I mean to say — he's right, he is that. 'Stick to navigation', do you hear that, Mac?"

Gerrard was staring pointedly at Watson, and I realised that he suspected the giant navigator of manipulating both the occasion and the furniture to his own advantage. I only felt relief that the spirit had not counselled us to keep up the morning parades. The farmer lit an oil lamp, and McLaughlin rose to his feet, reaching for his forage-cap.

"The time has come when I feel the need of a little liquid refreshment. It's been a most interesting experience, madam, and we're extremely grateful to you. Knowing your habits, I don't suppose I can persuade you both to join us?"

He was correct in his assumption; the farmer and his wife were abstemious people, and declined the invitation. We squeezed ourselves into McLaughlin's four-seater and made our winding way to the White Hart at Lissington, while Watson boomed endorsement of the spirit's adjuration.

When winter came to Wickenby, we constantly ran out of coke, and the voracious stove stood cold and empty in our hut. Raids on the fuel stores of other huts were likely to be brutally repulsed. By February, all the chairs and most of the towel-stands and shelves had been broken up and burned. The warm flying-clothing, which was intended to withstand the cold winds over Germany, served another purpose in warding off the damp draughts of Lincolnshire. The styles of night-wear were as varied as the standards of personal hygiene, but at least nobody at Wickenby quite achieved the decadence of my erstwhile room-mate, Mugsy Johnson, who went fully dressed to bed.

The incidence of illness among the aircrews was low during the time that we spent on the squadron. Walker missed one trip, white recovering from the concussion which he suffered on the Hamburg trip, and Fairbairn and I each had a cold that kept us on the ground for a day or two. Apart from these instances, we lost no flying time through sickness, and the other crews maintained equally good health. We were lucky to stay reasonably clear of head colds, as clogged sinuses could be a serious matter for an airman. The increasing atmospheric pressure on descent from altitude caused an imbalance on either side of the aural membrane and, if the nasal passages were blocked, the normal methods of equalising the pressure, such as swallowing, yawning or shouting, didn't work. The mounting pressure then was very painful. Cassidy and I both carried an inhaler to help keep the sinuses clear, and I was usually able to clear my ears by holding my nose and blowing hard; this seemed to work all right, but I was told that the method could cause damage, and it wasn't recommended by the doctor.

The MO was around if needed, and was always to be seen at briefing, handing out caffeine tablets to those of us who needed them. Later I heard about issues of benzedrine pills, which were supposed to provide a boost over the target, if such a stimulus were needed, but I saw no signs of these at Wickenby. We required no drug to alert us at that point; nature's adrenalin was quite enough, oozing from its glands, to stiffen the sleepy sinews, and summon up the sluggish blood.

Apart from the caffeine treatment, we didn't bother the MO much. We troubled the padre even less. He was a cheerful, bespectacled man, with whom we might have had a closer contact under normal circumstances, but he wore a squadron leader's uniform, which seemed an irrelevance to me and gave him an exclusive status which I didn't think he'd want. I felt that, if he had to wear a uniform, it should have been either without a rank badge, or should have shown a higher rank than any on the station.

It was true that ranks in Bomber Command were one step (in PFF two steps) above their normal standing. Thus, a Squadron Leader led a flight, a Wing Commander commanded a squadron, and a Group Captain, although he led the station, captained no group, which was commanded by an Air Vice Marshal. As far as I knew, the padre had in his command one airman clerk, so he really rated no more than the rank of IAC or Corporal, if his ratings were to be based on responsibility for personnel. However, if he was considered, as God's vicar, to be responsible for us all, Air Commodore was the rank he should have held. Then we Pilot Officers could have told him, "we one-ringers ought to stick together," like the character in a current magazine cartoon.

Some of the movies we saw, which dramatised other battles, showed some earnest priest blessing the troops before they went into the fray. At least we suffered no such hypocritical performance; if you wanted to attend the tiny makeshift station church, you could; if not, your only contact with the padre would be to accept a mug of cocoa, or a tot of rum from him at the debriefing.

Lanham's commission soon followed mine, and he missed the next two operations while on outfitting leave. His turret seat was occupied on successive nights by Jimmy Strachan, a Canadian gunner who was temporarily without a crew. We went with sixteen others from the squadron to Kassel on 3 October, taking off at 1842hrs in JB354 Oboe. The route to the target was bent like a dog's hind leg to incorporate two feint attacks which, the Command tacticians hoped, would so confuse the enemy controllers that the night-fighters would all be patrolling the wrong place when we arrived over Kassel. We aimed firstly at Hanover, but thirty miles short turned south-west as if we were going to one of the Ruhr targets, and finally made another sharp turn to head south-east for Kassel.

The sky was clear of cloud and, at 2133hrs, Myring aimed without difficulty at a target-indicator burning on the ground, where many fires were burning fiercely. Two minutes later, the whole area was illuminated by a vast explosion, and Myring was enraptured:

"Cripes, skip, did you see that? My oath, what a bloody great bang! I reckon I got a bull's-eye."

The feint attacks, although they lengthened the sortie time to six hours and a quarter, seemed to have hindered the defences. We saw no fighters over Kassel and, without their interference, the attack appeared to be well concentrated.

The next night we took another Mark III Lancaster, JA922 Jig Two, to Frankfurt am Main. We had trouble starting her, and the other eighteen squadron aircraft were on their way to Beachy Head before we got off the ground, well past the deadline. However, Jig Two responded gallantly to urging. and we had caught up with the tail-end of the stream by the time we crossed the Channel. From the French coast, above the Somme estuary, we set course direct for Mannheim. When we turned off to the north-east for Frankfurt, a small diversionary force continued straight ahead to make a spoof attack on Mannheim. We slightly overshot our turning-point, and found ourselves ploughing through the full extent of the massive searchlight belt that stretched between the two cities. Both gunners and the bomb-aimer kept me well informed about the threat of the questing searchlight fingers, and between us we contrived to fly through them for forty miles without permitting one to fasten on Jig Two. The exercise made me sweat so much that I had to have the cabin heat turned off. The others stoically forbore to complain about the cold.

As with Kassel on the night before, the attack seemed to be highly concentrated. Hutchinson's aircraft was damaged by flak over the target, and one crew returned early, but the squadron had no losses. Indeed, two crews finished their tours, and it was comforting to know that some people actually made it to that distant thirty-operations mark.

The tours of two Canadian gunners were terminated less auspiciously. They had been at briefing but, as take-off time drew near, they were nowhere to be found. The Tannoy bleated for them all over Wickenby without result. Two stand-by gunners were unearthed, and hurriedly prepared; the last one scrambled into the Lancaster as it rolled past the watchtower on the way to take-off.

The runaways eventually returned to face the inevitable court martial, and it was ordained, perhaps *pour encourager les autres*, that the sentence be pronounced before us all. On a cool, grey morning the full complement of Wickenby was mustered by flights and squadrons on the parade ground. The ritual proceeded normally at first; dressing by Flights, Flights number, stand at ease. The Station Commander made his entrance, wearing his peaked cap with the "scrambled egg" instead of the usual faded forage-cap. Most of the young officers, when they faced a body of men on parade, looked either fierce or foolish; many indeed, contrived a mixture of the two, but Crummy had been around a very long time, and he looked reasonably at ease as he took his place in front of us.

"Parade, attention."

He turned about to face the flagstaff.

"General salute."

The orderly sergeant jerked the ensign to the head of the staff, following its progress anxiously with his eyes.

"Parade, open order march. Right dress. Eyes front. No. 1 Squadron, stand fast. Nos. 2 and 3 Squadron Commanders, inspect your squadrons."

We kept a semblance of rigidity while the Station Commander and his retinue made their slow progress through the ranks. At last they reached the last file of our rearmost rank, and exchanged salutes with our commander. When we had resumed close order, the drama of the day began. The miscreants were marched on to the parade ground from the left flank, and stationed between their escorts front and centre. In a formal, toneless voice, the Adjutant read out the charge against them, followed by the findings and the sentence of the court.

The ensign stirred limply on the staff. At the rear of No. 3 Squadron there was a quickly stilled disturbance as a fainting aircraftman was led away. As silence fell again, the Station Commander marched to one of the offenders and, with sure, quick movements, ripped the chevrons from each sleeve and the brevet from the breast. The gunner was a tall, aquiline fellow who might have stepped from a page of Longfellow's *Hiawatha*. He stood erect and motionless, staring straight ahead. The grey-blue sleeve showed darker where the tapes had been. The other gunner stood with shoulders bowed, and would not raise his eyes. He flinched at the Station Commander's touch. It was a dreadful moment.

Our transition to the officers' mess gave us a more personal contact with the characters of that company. The Station Commander himself had to be counted among the more eccentric of these. If I hadn't been commissioned, it's unlikely that I would ever have seen him eating glass, and I probably wouldn't have believed it if somebody had told me. After all, it was a thing that had to be seen to be believed. He took quite a long time to crunch it up, and he didn't talk much while he was doing it, but he ate a full-size wine-glass while I watched him, and never turned a hair. The MO was watching too, and he looked rather worried. He said:

"I hope you realise what you're doing, sir."

"Of course I do. Do you want to try it yourself?"

"I most certainly do not, sir. And I don't believe you know what you're doing to your insides."

Crummy ran his tongue over his lips and smiled.

"I know I could do with a drink, doc, if you're interested."

The MO knocked on the serving hatch.

"Steward, a large Scotch for the CO, please. No, seriously, sir, that glass you've been swallowing is going to build up a fine solution of arsenic when it meets your tummy acids."

Crummy raised an eyebrow at him.

"Arsenic? That's a poison."

"It is, indeed. How long have you been practising this little trick, sir, may I ask?"

"Oh, a long time. I picked it up from a chap I was with in Iraq. That'd be — what? 1927, I suppose."

The MO looked at him with a wondering expression, and shook his head.

"Hm. Quite extraordinary. What the system will stand, I mean. Good health, sir. And I really mean that."

The Station Commander chuckled, and picked up his drink.

"All right, doc. I must admit you had me worried for a minute. Cheers."

The MO was slightly offended.

"Believe me, sir, I'm perfectly serious. I don't joke about matters of medicine."

"Balls."

"Now look here, sir, do you know what the constituents of glass are? Because . . ."

I left them to sort it out, for I had noticed that another member of the mess was trying to drink a pint of beer, while at the same time balancing another on his head. This was Jumbo, the deputy Gunnery Leader, a long-legged fellow with an engaging, confidential manner. He had a smooth, pink face, and a pair of ears which spread almost enough to get him airborne when he cycled into wind. He also had a large revolver and a dangerous sense of humour. It was his favourite diversion to break into a fellow officer's bedroom in the early hours, affecting an advance stage of boozy bellicosity and brandishing the loaded pistol carelessly. Shouting of some imaginary grievance, he would then take a wavering aim at the cringing occupant and, after a few suspenseful moments, fire a round or two through an adjacent window. If the window happened to be open, no great harm was done, except to his victim's nervous system; if it were closed, the price of a new pain had to be added to the cost of the amusement.

Jumbo's senior, the Squadron Gunnery Leader, was conscious of the possibility that the joker's bullet might some night fly past his own head. Sure enough, the moment came when Wilkie's door flew open, and the expected firearm waved towards him. Without a word, Wilkie produced a heavy automatic from beneath his pillow and, aiming it between the intruder's eyes, steadily thumbed back the safety catch. As his forefinger tightened on the trigger, Jumbo, suddenly as sober in act as he was in fact, dived through the door and landed in the corridor on his face. Wilkie replaced the automatic under his pillow, and called after his visitor:

"Good-night, Jumbo. Oh, you might shut the door, there's a good chap."

There was no need for Jumbo and his gun to frighten me: I was fully capable of frightening myself. We were climbing high through thin cloud one evening, when came one of those frights which, though minor, you know you never will forget. Half hidden in the luminous mist, there appeared a sudden moving shape, level on the port bow. It was an aircraft like our own, dim, but yes, surely a heavy bomber on a converging course, and coming close. With adrenalin coursing to my muscles, I hauled the wheel and kicked the rudders left, to pass behind and rise above it. It turned too, towards me.

Gasping, I wrenched the wheel the other way, forced the nose down steeply, and trod hard on the starboard rudder. Looming vast, the monster did the same. With every nerve-end tingling, I realised the truth. We met the chimera in head-on collision, and it broke into a sheen of water vapour as the sky turned blue. The sinking western sun had thrown a shadow, and my half-sleeping eyes had made it substance. With mingling relief and shame, I made confession to the crew.

"Sorry about the aerobatics — I was dodging our reflection on the cloud. Back on course now."

★   ★   ★

As magnetic as the phantom *Lancaster*, though less ephemeral, was one of the WAAF transport drivers at Wickenby. She was a slim, dark-haired girl with sad eyes, who had bad luck with her boyfriends. A pilot and a gunner who were close to her went missing, and when she turned to a civil engineer in the Works Department, he was quickly killed in a motor-cycle accident on the airfield. The word went round that the lady was a jinx, but to me she seemed to have a tragic glamour. I approached her boldly, and we made a date. Ten minutes before we were due to meet, a Tannoy broadcast told me to report to the Navigation Leader at his place of work. Five minutes later, I was alone in the silent map room, and the door was locked on the outside. A clerk released me after fifty minutes; he said he had no idea who might have locked me in and the Navigation Leader, when I challenged him, swore that he had made no Tannoy call. I would have liked to lay that jinx, but mine was a jealous crew, and perhaps a little superstitious, too.

Much of the airman's ethos, if not exactly superstitious, was of necessity based on faith, and sometimes that faith was unsupported, as when it was placed in wishful intelligence assessments, in unreliable or outdated weapons, and in invisible commanders. But sometimes it had a firmer basis: the skid of the ground crews, the care of the controllers, the courage of the air-sea rescue men and, far from least, the strength of the aircraft's components and systems.

Certainly, the Rolls-Royce engines rarely gave us reason for concern; they churned on hour after hour, apparently immune to the effects of rain, snow, hail or sleet. On the way to Stuttgart, however, on the night of 7 October, Merlin's magic failed for once. As Charlie Two approached the French coastline, the port outer wreathed itself in flames. The flight engineer was in a peaceful doze, his chin sunk on his chest. I tapped him on the shoulder and pointed at the burning engine. As he stared at it, his mouth fell open, and I saw the flames reflected in his eyes. I watched him fight to break the spell in which the shock was holding him, and then his hands moved fast. He closed the throttle, and his right forefinger stabbed the feathering button as his left hand shut the fuel cock. The propeller windmilled, stopped, and Walker pressed the button of the fire-extinguisher. After a few anxious moments, the flames dwindled and died. I wound the trimming-wheels to balance the drag of the dead engine, and told the navigator what had happened.

"We'll be five mph slower, maybe more. I'll let you know, when she settles down."

"You're going on to Stuttgart on three?"

"We'd see how it goes."

"Okay. I'll give you a new course when your airspeed's steady."

But Charlie Two had no intention of reaching Stuttgart that night. Soon the port inner began to surge unpleasantly, and within moments it was over-revving and windmilling alternately, with temperatures climbing high into the danger zone. The aircraft stewed from side to side, and the altimeter needle moved anti-clockwise as she lost height. I pulled another throttle back.

"Feather port inner."

"Feathering port inner."

"I'm turning back. Nav, give me a course for base. Bomb-aimer, when we're over water let the bombs go."

As we crept back, crabwise, towards the English Channel, steadily losing height, I realised that Wickenby might be beyond our reach. We needed some runway, and we needed it soon.

We arrived over the night-fighter base at West Malting in low cloud, poor visibility, and a small-scale air-raid. I had practised a few landings on three engines, but none on two. The drill for three-engined landings was that you always made the circuit turning away from the bad engine, so that you could keep control of the turns, and prevent the asymmetric power from taking over. I figured that a similar technique would apply in the case of two-engined landings, only more so. With both port engines out of use, I should have to make a right-hand circuit instead of the usual left-hander.

I found that I had to use a lot more rudder than I had expected to persuade Charlie Two to turn right, and at the first attempt I didn't give myself sufficient room to get on to a good approach path. Then I noticed that I'd forgotten to take the engines out of the fully supercharged gear that we used for high altitude. One way or another, I made a mess of that approach.

"Unfeather the port inner, Johnny. It might help a bit on these starboard turns. But watch the temperatures."

We lurched round West Malting again. On the next approach I brought her down lower. Too low, too slow, and always left of the runway. No good.

"Wheels up. I have the throttles. Milk the flap off gently."

The accelerating engines roared angrily. Charlie Two crept across the dark airfield, still losing height. She gained a little airspeed in a dip beyond the runway, and clawed her way slowly up to safer air. Safer, that is, so long as there were no double-decker buses on our track.

"Jeez, skip, good job you missed that hill — we've still got the incendiaries on board."

"What?"

"Yeah, I only dropped the HEs off in the Channel. I thought we'd save something for tomorrow."

"You thought . . . never mind. We'll drop the lot as soon as we can find some sea."

We slid through the black drizzle, never gaining height, found the coast and dropped a dozen canisters of fire bombs into the inky water. Plodding back to West Malting, I found that I had lost faith in the right-hand-circuit school of thought. I sat up straight, took a piece of the engineer's chewing-gum, and positioned Charlie Two for a normal left-hand circuit on the long runway.

"Okay, third time lucky, wheels down."

"She'll be right this time, skip."

Charlie Two sidled down the approach, levelled out with the starboard wing down, touched starboard wheel first with a squeal, then touched the port wheel on concrete, and she was down. I found a convenient hard-standing, and switched off. Fire engines, trucks and an ambulance appeared out of the darkness. We clambered out and stood under the port wing, sheltering from the rain, and examining the blackened engines.

"That's our first abortive."

"Who woulda thought old Charlie Two would let us down?"

"Where is this place?"

A flight truck pulled up, and from it an Irving-jacketed figure approached us. I distinguished a fair-haired man, wearing an officer's forage-cap, and moved forward to meet him. I asked:

"Are you on duty?"

"On duty? Yes. Yes, I'm on duty."

"Right, now listen. I was here about six months ago, diverted on a right cross-country from OTU. There were no sheets on the beds, and we couldn't get a hot meal in the mess. Pretty poor show. See what you can do, will you?"

The officer's bright, blue eyes looked into mine. He smiled slightly.

"Who are you?"

"Currie — Pilot Officer Currie. I'm the captain."

"I see. You want sheets on your beds?"

"Yes. Clean sheets."

"And a meal?"

"Hot meals."

"I'll see what I can do."

"Good man."

A truck took us to the tower, and I told the people there what had happened to Charlie Two. The intelligence officer plotted the places where we had dropped the bombs, then looked up and smiled at me.

"My God, when you came in the second time and disappeared into the dip at the end of the runway, we all put our fingers in our ears."

"So did we."

"By the way, did you see 'Cat's-eyes'?"

"What size?"

"Cat's-eyes Cunningham — our CO."

"No."

"Oh, pity. He went out to meet you."

"Oh. Not a fellow in an Irving jacket, is he?"

"That's right."

"Oh, dear."

Clean sheets and hot food we had, and night-fighter ace Cunningham opened the bar, and poured us a drink himself. As I told the navigator, it's always best to talk to the top man.

Next morning, we found that both the port engines would have to be stripped down, and that there was no chance of taking the aircraft back to Wickenby for several days. Charlie Lanham wrote on a piece of paper, "Only carrots to eat here send help", took the homing-pigeon from its box in the fuselage, and put the message in the capsule on its foot. He pointed the bird northwards, and released it with a shout of encouragement. It made a laboured circuit, and alighted on a nearby hangar roof.

"Get airborne, pigeon!"

"Get homing, you idle bird."

"Steer three-six-oh."

"Chuck a stone at it."

The pigeon flapped further along the roof.

"Maybe it's tour-expired."

"Nah — you can't finish on an abortive."

I went to find the orderly room. We hadn't a penny between us, and we needed travel warrants to get us back to base.

While we travelled on the train to Lincoln, the squadron's crews were briefed for Hanover. Two of them did not return, and Rowland's rear-gunner was killed. Then fog enveloped Wickenby in such a close embrace that even the birds were still. We took six days of our leave entitlement, and missed the next two operations, when the squadron made a repeat trip to Hanover on 18 October, and went to Kassel four nights later. Three of the unlucky Rowlands crew were injured when his aircraft was hit again, and Lloyd's crew was missing from the second mission.

The Fortress came in on three engines, with some battle-damage and a wounded gunner, and parked in a "B" flight dispersal. We walked out to inspect the stranger in the mottled camouflage paint. It sat lower to the ground than our black Lancasters, and the rounded nose, sweeping tail-fairing and radial engines presented a less aggressive profile. We admired the fire-power, and the comfort of the cockpit. We also liked the vivid picture of a naked lady, which was painted on the nose.

We were on stand-down that night, and so were free to fraternise with the American officers in the mess. It wasn't easy; they stood together, silent, wearing their flying-boots and leather jackets. I saw the tired, pale faces and the worried eyes with sympathy and some surprise, remembering all those stalwart cadets who strode in the Georgia sunshine, and sang "Nothing can stop the Army Air Corps". These boys looked as though they might tell you what you could do with the "wide, blue yonder" of the song. I walked over and touched the elbow of one of the pilots.

"How's the gunner?"

"Not so good."

"What hit him?"

"Cannon shell. In the foot."

"That's bad."

"Likely to lose his leg."

"Poor chap."

"Yeah."

"Care for a drink?"

"I guess not."

After dinner, the atmosphere was a little more relaxed. I tried again.

"How about that drink now?"

"I don't believe so. I guess we ought to hit the sack."

"Come on! Do you good."

"Well . . ."

We had a few bottles of pale ale, and exchanged polite comparisons of the Lancaster and the B17. The wine was flowing in one corner, and some of my colleagues had reached the singing stage.

Old King Cole was a merry old soul, and a
    merry old soul was he,
He called for his kites in the middle of the night,
    and he called for his pilots three.
Every pilot was a fine type, and a very fine type
    was he.
"I don't give a f . . ." said the pilot, "merry,
    merry men are we, There's none so rare as can
    compare with the boys of Wickenby."
Old King Cole was a merry old soul . . .

The American pilot and I leaned against the bar. I
had to raise my voice to be heard above the singing.

"I was trained in the States."

"Is that right?"

"The Arnold Scheme — 'Marching through
Georgia', and all that."

"The deep south, huh? Where'd you graduate?"

"Moody Field."

"Valdosta?"

"That's right. D'you know it?"

. . . and he called for his engineers three.
Every engineer was a fine type, and a very fine
    type was he: "I want four pounds boost," said
    the engineer, "I don't give a f . . ." said the
    pilot, "merry, merry men are we . . ."

The padre put his head round the ante-room door,
smiled as he recognised the song, and withdrew. The
American sipped his beer warily.

"Did you get to meet a guy called Carlson — Cap'n Carlson?"

"The army check pilot? I had a check ride with him once."

"Man, he was one hard-assed bastard."

"Wasn't he, though?"

Every bomb-aimer was a fine type, and a very
    fine type was he:
"Left, left, steady — dummy run" said the
    bomb-aimer.
"I want four pounds boost," said the
    engineer . . .

"I held the RAF record for demerits in the States."

"That right? How many?"

"A hundred and eighty in six months. We were allowed three a week — every one over that, you watched a one-hour tour."

"That's a lotta walking, boy."

"I collected fifty in one go, at primary."

"What did you do, screw the Colonel's daughter?"

"They told me there were crocodiles in the Flint River — I was trying to find one."

"Caught low-flying?"

"By the Chief Instructor. Lucky not to get washed out."

. . . "Dah-di-di-dah di-di-dah," said the wireless-
    op,
"We are bang on track," said the navigator, "Left,

left, steady — dummy run," said the bomb-
    aimer,
"I want four pounds boost," said the engineer, "I
    don't give a f . . ." said the pilot, "merry,
    merry men are we,
There's none so rare as can compare . . ."

The American ordered more pale ale, and put a
ten-shilling note on the bar. I was glad that he seemed
to be getting the flavour.

"That sonofabitch 109 flew right in through the
whole goddam formation, head-on."

"Did you see his face?"

"Pardon me?"

"The Jerry pilot — did you see his face?"

"Man, I could see the colour of his eyes!"

"I had this 210 on Peenemunde . . ."

Somebody was beating his tankard on a table to the
rhythm of the song, and the other three visitors seemed
to be picking up the words quite well.

. . . and he called for his mid uppers three.
Every mid-upper was a fine type, and a very fine
    type was he:
"Corkscrew port like hell," said the mid-upper,
"Dah-di-di-dah di-di-dah," said the wireless-
    op . . .

"That's Mary Lou, second from the left."

"Very pretty."

"The guys think she kinda looks like Lana Turner."

"So she does."

"Down the hatch!"

"Cheers!"

We turned back to the bar. The noise swelled as the singers, tunics unbuttoned and eyes glazed in an ecstasy of self-appreciation, drove mercilessly on to their final chorus.

> Old King Cole was a merry old soul, and a
>   merry old soul was he.
> He called for his kites in the middle of the night,
>   and he called for his rear-gunners three.
> Every rear-gunner was a fine type, and a very
>   fine type was he:
> "Jesus Christ, it's cold," said the rear-gunner,
> "Corkscrew port like hell," said the mid-upper,
> "Dah-di-di-dah di-di-dah," said the wireless-op,
> "We are bang on track," said the navigator,
> "Left, left, steady — dummy run," said the
>   bomb-aimer,
> "I want four pounds boost," said the engineer,
> "I don't give a f . . ." said the pilot, "merry,
>   merry men are we,
> There's none so rare as can compare with the
>   boys of Wickenby."

Charlie Two moved smoothly westward, occasionally veering from her course, and being gently corrected. The land and sky were of an equal blackness; the stars hung steady in their complicated pattern, suggesting the horizon by the line at which they ceased.

"Mid-upper to skipper — permission to leave the turret?"

"What for, George?"

"I want to leave the turret for a few minutes."

"Yes — I said what for?"

"Well, er — I think I've shit myself, skipper."

"What do you mean, you think? Are you ill?"

"No, I've just shit myself. I thought I was farting, but I wasn't."

I imagined little George, squirming in his electrically heated suit, and an unkind demon prompted my reply.

"There are five hundred night-fighters looking for us, mid-upper, and it's up to you to stop them. I can't let you leave the turret yet."

"Oh. Okay, skipper."

Comment crackled on the intercom.

"Too many baked beans, George."

"Too much beer, more like."

"Let it bake, mid-upper."

Two hours later, the North Sea rolled below us, and I remembered George's problem.

"Pilot to mid-upper. Okay to leave the turret now, but make it snappy."

"Thanks all the same, skipper, I won't bother."

"Why not? Don't you want to clean up?"

"No, it's okay. It's gone hard."

We gave the shame-faced George a wide berth back at Wickenby, and wouldn't let him sit near us in the crew bus.

Protheroe's little accident had its element of comedy, if not to say of farce, but now a time of tragedy

155

darkened Myring's life. His Freda gave birth to a son, and for several days he beamed and bristled with happy pride, immersing himself in quantities of beer "to wet the baby's head", while autumn mist lay damp and heavy on the fields, and the spectral Lancasters stayed silent at their sodden stations. Then a telegram told Larry that Freda was ill, the baby dying. He left, dulled by hangover and horror, to be with them.

My mother sent her sympathy for Larry and her blessings to the crew. She enclosed money and asked if it were possible for me to obtain any eggs, honey or marmalade or jam, soap vouchers, Yardley's vanishing cream or Velouty powder-cream, ham or bacon, apples, and a chicken. Great Aunt Alice wrote of her interest in my exploits, and reminded me of my responsibilities as captain of a crew. My bank manager confided in me of his concern about the state of my account, and wondered whether I might find it possible to maintain it on a credit basis. Three lovely girls sent me their love, and mentioned that they were looking forward to my next leave. I shared their view, and thought of them. Of Beryl, with the crisp blonde curls and firm, slim body like a boy, star of suburban tennis courts. Of the dance-band singer, feline Kay, smooth-haired, soft-skinned, making sexy wisecracks in her snappy London accent. And of Celtic Muriel, from the Shrewsbury telephone exchange, with her thick black hair and deep-throated laughter, whose proper lover wished me dead.

But now the mists rolled back, and the Lancasters stood dripping in the sheen of slanting sunlight. Charlie

Two, with two new engines, had been returned from Kent, and on 3 November we prepared her for a raid on Düsseldorf.

The savage fates had followed Myring's trail; the train in which he travelled back to Lincoln had been derailed, his carriage overturned. He had extricated himself and five more passengers, and arrived at Wickenby in time for briefing. The exhaustion in his face, and the damage to his hands, shadowed my joy at his return. I put my hand on his shoulder.

"You can't fly, Larry. Go and get your head down."

"I'm bloody well coming with you. You can't stop me."

But I did. Bluey Turner was detailed to deputise, while Larry slept.

Charlie Two climbed strongly in the cool evening air and, when we turned north-east for the bombing run, she had reached 21,500 feet. The sky was free of cloud, and the visibility was very good above a thin ground haze which lay across Rhineland. 2,000 tons of bombs fell in twenty-seven minutes on a strangely subdued Düsseldorf. In such a concentrated stream of aircraft some accidents were bound to happen, and it was Bluey Turner's unhappy lot to let his bombs go a split second before a Halifax, several thousand feet below, drifted in between his sight wires. A merciful bloom of shell-smoke hid the outcome from his view. The time was ten minutes to eight, and an hour and three-quarters later we were back at Wickenby. Two new squadron crews did not return.

★　★　★

By daylight, Lincoln was an easy place to find from the air. The rule-straight Roman roads, Ermine Street and the Fosse Way, pointed from the north and the south-west; the railway lines meandered in from all directions; from Market Rasen, Louth and Boston, from Sleaford, Grantham, Newark and from Gainsborough. The stonework of the great cathedral shone softly in the sunlight, and the majestic structure seemed to float upon the city, above the fields of Lindsey and Kesteven. The sight of it, serene and monumental, imbued me with inchoate thoughts of England's past, and of our little part in working for her future sovereignty.

Young men had come from the far ends of the world to join us on the airfields lying round Lincoln: from Canada and India, Australia and New Zealand, Rhodesia and South Africa. I didn't know what moved them; was it a sense of duty, love of the old country, Commonwealth, Empire, democracy? Perhaps a hatred of tyranny or dictatorship, perhaps a zest for danger, who knew? We were subject to the general intake of patriotic exhortations, some stirring, some silly, like everybody else. Winston Churchill strove to stimulate the people's spirits with his speeches, bellicose and sibilant. Chauvinistic songs, less inspiring than embarrassing, often beat upon our ears. Noel Coward wrote a poem about us bomber crews, called "Lie in the dark and listen", which was succinct and stylish but carried no great significance and was slightly blush-making. Actors depicted us as leather-muffled public schoolboys, stiffening our upper lips in studio cockpits among the phoney flak bursts.

On the other side, the Nazi propagandist Dr Goebbels called us "terror-fliers" and "hired assassins of the King", terms which chimed more with the latent love of violence in us than did the sentimental soubriquets of song and cinema, or the Army's scornful "Brylcreem Boys".

Largely unmoved by exhortation, praise or condemnation, I satisfied what need I had for motivation by the companionship of the men from far-off lands around me, and the sight of the cathedral and the wide, green fields.

CHAPTER
SEVEN

The New Squadron Forms

Some administrative reorganisation now took place. We of "C" flight were removed from 12 Squadron, and became the nucleus of a new Wickenby squadron, numbered 626. We took our eight bombers with us, and received a further eight so that, instead of accommodating one squadron of three flights and twenty-four aircraft, Wickenby now had two squadrons, each of two flights, and sixteen aircraft. By this time, we had accumulated sufficient seniority to command the allocation of our own particular aircraft, so we took Charlie Two to 626 Squadron with us, and the dusky red code letters PH on her fuselage were amended to UM.

At Modane, the railway ran from Grenoble to Turin deep under the Graian Alps. Through the tunnel, German reinforcements passed from France to threatened Italy. Our task on 10 November, flying our Charlie Two on 626 Squadron's first operation, was to block the tunnel. To this end, we carried a cookie and five 1,000 pounders to the target, which lay 1600 miles from Wickenby.

We arrived early in the target area, and circled high among the Alpine peaks, gazing at magnificent Mont Blanc, towering massive in the moonlight, with our target to the south and Lake Geneva to the north. When our time-on-target came, we moved in straight and level, without a hostile shot to shake our calm. The tunnel entrance was clearly illuminated by a combination of PFF flares, high explosive and full moonlight. The veriest duffer with a bomb-sight should have got pretty close to that inviting target. Myring was no duffer, and he hit it on the nose.

Our oxygen supply ran out on the way home over France, and we therefore crossed the coast much lower than we planned. At this unscheduled level, we were lucky to miss a Mosquito, coming at us on a head-on course, by a few brief feet.

A heavy front was cutting off the moonlight over England, and we struggled home below the ragged cloud-base, bouncing and vibrating at 2,000 feet.

Such bumpy passages must have been upsetting to a queasy stomach, and I was thankful that mine was unaffected by turbulence. Nausea seemed to strike in unexpected ways; I remembered Mugsy Johnson, who was never troubled in the air, but who turned a nasty shade of green at the gentle rocking of a troopship in the Clyde. Many an airman had a weakness that he had to learn to live with, sometimes of a sort that made it hard to live with him. Such a one flew with our squadron.

The trouble with Tony was that he passed wind involuntarily and heavily. He was a pilot, with the rank of flying officer, and he was engaged in two wars at the same time. One was our common fight against the Axis powers, and the other, more personal, was his perpetual struggle with the demon drink. It appeared to be his objective to drink all the bitter beer in Lincolnshire, before it killed him, and he never spared himself in his efforts to achieve his aim. The barman at the officers' mess had instructions to place a full tankard on the counter at twelve thirty every day. Within a few moments, Tony would lurch into the bar and, not lifting, but tilting the tankard towards himself with quivering hands, would crouch over the counter to sink his moustache into the foam. Pausing for breath, he would mutter:

"I'll beat you yet, you bastard!"

Then, standing erect, and holding the pot to his lips with both hands, he would savagely imbibe the rest of the ale. It was at this point that Tony's gut would begin to make its aerated presence known, and those of us who were acquainted with the form would remove ourselves to a safe distance, while the noxious fumes escaped. After the third or fourth pint, Tony's hands would stop shaking, his eyes would focus, and the air would clear. It was then possible to approach, and pass the time of day with him, without fear of contamination.

We learned that similar symptoms announced themselves whenever Tony's Lancaster was climbing for altitude over Wickenby. As the air became thinner with height, so his intolerable gases expanded. His cabin crew were accustomed to use emergency oxygen from ground level, in their determination to retain consciousness.

I referred Tony's case to Lanham, in rebuttal of the gunner's theory that drink and flying didn't mix.

"How do you explain it, Charlie? This chap lives on beer, but he keeps coming back for more ops."

Lanham stared at me bleakly.

"You wanna be like him? You can start looking for another rear-gunner right now."

"I didn't say I wanted to be like him. But his way of life certainly doesn't square with your grog-means-the-chop theory."

"Listen, Jack. Don't you know the score? That crew never goes to the target. They just fly round in circles over the sea until it's time to come home."

I laughed at him.

"You don't believe that, dig. How about the bomb-release photograph? What about the navigator's log?"

"All fixed. They bribe the nav and bombing leaders with chocolates and clothing-coupons."

On 22 November we opened the winter campaign against the German capital or, as our masters were to call it, "The Battle of Berlin". The mission took six and a half hours, three of which were spent in heavy cloud. Charlie Two's airspeed indicator was rendered useless as we left the target, by icing of the pitot tube. Fortunately, the ice melted three hours later, when we came down to circuit height over Wickenby, and so I had a reading when I carried out the landing. A certain Sergeant Jackson, on his second-dicky trip, sat beside me on the engineer's seat, while the long suffering Walker stood patiently behind him through the night. The new boy's comment, "The flak's not very impressive, is it?" came brightly, as we were struggling through the robust defences of Hanover, and greatly cheered us all. I remembered my own inclination to whistle in the dark, when I had been in his position, and forgave him.

It seemed a long, long time since that first trip of mine, and still nine missions lay between us and the finish of our tour. Nine others such as this, crouching in the roaring, frozen darkness, glaring at a useless instrument, wondering if even now another bomber converged upon us on collision course. Perhaps the flak pattern was creeping up behind us, radar-directed, and we couldn't see it. There were no stars to calm the nerves, with their eternal steadfast symmetry, no horizon to aim at, no gleam of coast or river to establish some relation with the earth. It was absolute isolation. I wanted to hear the voices of the crew for their companionship, but I daren't encourage them to talk in case they broke my concentration. Now the thought came that the effort was beyond me, that I had done enough. I would go to the CO next morning, and tell him so. To carry on was certain suicide — they were bound to get us in the end. I warmed myself for several minutes with the thought of the release from danger, but then the navigator broke into my dream.

164

"Make it two-six-five degrees, Jack, will you?"

"Two-six-five."

As I swung the wheel and twitched the rudders, I thought of Cassidy. What of him, without met I thought of Lanham, of Fairbairn, Myring, Walker, Protheroe. What of them? I remembered exchanging glances with the rear-gunner back at Wickenby, after our first real brush with danger, when we both realised together that we were in a very rough game. I had said:

"What do you say we put in for eighteen months' deferred service?"

Lanham had smiled, then grinned, then roared with laughter. "Come on, Currie," I thought, "you yellow bastard. Straighten up and fly right, you're supposed to be an ace."

Next night, the target was Berlin again. We made the trip in five hours and fifty minutes, which was our best time for the big city. The speed was attributable to the fact that the airspeed indicator was iced up again, this time from take-off to landing, and I must have instinctively kept the knots well on the safe side of the stall. The route was the same as last night's, but this time we met heavy, accurate flak over Texel on the coast-crossings in and out. We were hit in the fuselage on the way home, when we were flying in thick cloud at 20,000 feet. The weather became steadily worse, and we suffered an hour of rough treatment in the grip of an occlusion, as we returned at 1,500 feet above the North Sea.

As I brought Charlie Two into the airfield traffic pattern over Wickenby, Lanham caged me on the intercom.

"How's the ASI, Jack?"

"Still iced up — no reading."

"Can you judge the airspeed for the landing all right?"

"Blowed if I know. I'll have a try."

"I can tell you what your airspeed is on the approach, if you like."

That surprised me. The navigator had the only other ASI in the aircraft, and that was simply a repeater of mine, taking its reading from the same blocked pitot-tube. I asked the rear-gunner:

"How can you tell the airspeed, Charlie?"

"By the noise of the slipstream in the turret. I know what speeds you usually do, and I know what it sounds like back here."

I thumped the useless dial with my gloved knuckles. Walker grinned, and shook his head. Lanham's estimate could well be helpful — his sense of airmanship was sound.

"Okay, rear-gunner, give it a go."

I turned on to the final approach at 800 feet, with the undercarriage down, and a third of the flap, rpm levers high and zero boost. I headed the nose at the pathway of flares, and took the throttle levers into my right hand.

"Give me half flap, Johnny. Let's hear from you, Charlie."

"It sounds about right, Jack. A hundred and twenty-five . . . a hundred and twenty-five . . . a hundred and twenty . . ."

The figures reported by the gunner approximately agreed with my own guesswork. They can't have been far out, because we made a good approach, and a better landing than usual. One of the 12 Squadron aircraft did not come back.

As a result of these successive sorties to Berlin, a newly arrived sergeant-pilot came to grief. He was a casualty neither of flak nor fighters, but of an enemy within himself. He came back early from the mission on 22 November, and gave as a reason the fact that he was feeling ill. Next night he took off again, but was back over Wickenby twenty minutes later. Again, he said that he had felt ill in the air. I had seen the crew together in the locker-room, clustered protectively around their white-faced pilot. They may have thought that some of us would vilify him, but no one except officialdom did that. We knew what was wrong: the so-called lack of moral fibre, and most of us had felt that at times.

I recalled the twitching gunner who met us when we first arrived at Wickenby. Lanham had seen him off, because he feared we might, in our inexperience, become infected by the frightened man's defeatism. Now we knew enough to take a tolerant view. But ours was not the attitude which counted; the Service said he must be disciplined. We were volunteers in aircrew but having volunteered, been trained and got our wings, there was no going back. A pilot's training cost a lot of money, and no nation in the crunch of war could waste a trained man with impunity. Goodness knows what hell the wretched pilot lived through — the fear of showing cowardice is the strongest fear of all in most young men. Soon he disappeared, posted to some dread unit especially established to cater for such unhappy cases.

Meanwhile, another Berlin operation of 26 November, from which my crew was excepted, cost both Wickenby squadrons crews and aircraft. From 12 Squadron, the Australian Bob Yell, a good friend of ours, and Sergeant Twitchett crashed on their return to base. Both survived on this occasion but as though their doom were written on the wall, failed to return from their next missions. Two Lancasters of 626 Squadron collided in the air, crashing fatally at nearby Lissington, and another crew was lost in a crash at Marham. We got used to accepting the casualties without overt reaction, and the sudden death of a friend evoked little more comment than, "Old Timber bought it last night, then?" and a grunted response. If it was your job to burn people's houses, knock down their places of work, stop their transport and blow up their gas mains, you had to expect some redress. It was best to ignore the losses and get on with the tour. Each in his fashion, we followed the routine of living in camp, with its scrounging and grumbles, its fun and frustrations.

On reading station routine orders one evening I noticed with concern that I was detailed to take the morning parade next day. This presented a challenge to the reputation I had won for avoiding such drab ceremonies. Again my luck held good, for a little machination set Jim Cassidy, spruce but scowling, on the parade ground in my place. When I saw him later in the flight office, his voice was strident with outrage.

"You bludger! You scroungers! You swung it on me, you rotten beggar!"

"Oh, come off it, Jimmy, you know you enjoy it. I was trying to do you a favour."

"You were what? I enjoy it! Aw, don't give us the horrors."

When the next operation was ordered, we knew from a glance at the weather chart that it was likely to be a nonstarter, and that we were in for a frustrating day. Sure enough, the mission was first postponed for a few hours and finally scrubbed, too late for it to be worth our while to go off camp. When I got to the mess, it was crowded, and the bar was doing a roaring trade. The medical officer was playing the piano for a group, led by "B" flight's commander, to sing a parody of "Bless 'em All".

"They say there's a Lancaster leaving the Ruhr,
Bound for old Blighty's shore.
Heavily laden with terrified men
All lying prone on the floor . . ."

Meanwhile, some of those officers whose proclivities were more muscular than musical were arranging the anteroom furniture in the form of an obstacle race. Face down on the carpet in the middle of the room lay two blindfolded officers, both senior and old enough to know better. They were indulging in the game called "Are you there, Moriarty?". Heads together and with left hands clasped, each took his turn to speak the formula; thereupon, the other might take a swingeing swipe with a rolled up newspaper at the point where he judged the speaker's head to be. Blows rained heavily on shoulders, heads and carpet as the protagonists squirmed and twisted. It would have been a good game for a heavy-handed ventriloquist, but not for me, and I persuaded a colleague to join me in a pseudo-hypnotic act which ended happily in the raised trouser-leg of a victim being filled with a pint of beer. The sound of the subsequent curses, and that of the choir at the piano, were now drowned by the roar of a high-revving engine. The swing doors from the entrance lobby were knocked apart by the front wheel of a heavy service motor-cycle. In the saddle sat the Station Commander, wearing his best blue and a blissful smile. He embarked on the first of several circuits around the anteroom, improving on his lap time at each attempt, and leaving a trail of scattered furniture and acrid exhaust fumes behind him as he moved off for a speed trial in the corridor. Unmoved, a four at bridge sat at a precarious table, fingering their cards as the *tricoteuses* handled their knitting-needles in the shadow of the guillotine.

When the MO took an intermission and refreshment at the piano, George Gerrard approached him, shaking horribly in every limb; his head spasmodically jerked sideways and, every few seconds, his left eye and the corner of his mouth twitched. He placed a trembling hand on the doctor's arm and croaked:

"I'll fly, Doc. Tell them I'm fit to fly. I was pretty bad this morning, but I'm okay now."

The MO, raising a tankard, glanced at him.

"Yes, you look all right to me."

"Gee, thanks, Doc."

Gerrard staggered away, alternately grimacing and twitching, and the choir, refreshed, struck up again to the tune of the German national anthem:

"Home presents a dismal picture, dark and
    dreary as the tomb;
Father has an anal stricture, mother has a
    prolapse womb,
Sister Mary has aborted for the forty-second
    time,
Brother Tom has been deported for a
    homosexual crime,
Little Willie's in the mad-house, Doctor says he's
    there for good,
And the cause of his affliction . . ."

And so on. Meanwhile, the obstacle racers were into their second lap, and bodies were flying in all directions. The tall figure of Jumbo, the gunnery expert, swayed towards me through the melee, and stooped to speak confidentially:

"Listen, old boy, you know I've just finished my second tour?"

"Yes, well played, Jumbo."

"Well, I'm posted tomorrow, and I want you to have something of mine to keep, something special."

"Oh?"

I was suspicious. The gunner was better known for his practical jokes than for his philanthropy. I looked into his eyes, but could see no tell-tale twinkle there. He seemed serious, even solemn, as he fumbled in the patch-pocket of his tunic.

"I reckon you're living on borrowed time since that Hamburg do of yours, and this might help you."

He produced a plain brass medallion, the size of a halfcrown. It was dented, slightly discoloured, and a safetypin had been stuck through a crudely pierced hole in the rim. Jumbo said:

"I've always worn it, every op."

He pushed the charm into my hand.

"Keep it in your pocket, or pin it on your blouse. Don't forget."

"Okay, Jumbo. Thanks a lot."

I watched him lurch away towards the bar, and wondered what impulse had made him single me out as the heir to his magic medallion. I had no lucky charm as such, although I always carried the key to my flying-clothing locker as a gesture of defiance, and sometimes a girl's silk stocking round my neck out of sentiment, but these weren't really mascots. Jumbo's medallion had guarded him for fifty operations; it must be powerful medicine.

When Jimmy Cassidy and I left the mess an hour or so later, we nearly bumped into the Station Commander coming in again. It was as well that we didn't, because this time he was driving the Hillman car. Fortunately for the mess furniture, the doorposts weren't quite wide enough and he couldn't get through, but it wasn't for want of trying. Although he failed in that particular project, Group Captain Crummy had his successes in matters of more moment. For example, he knew how tiresome it was for us to return from Germany on schedule only to spend anything up to an hour circling Wickenby in the darkness, waiting for a turn to land. The trouble was that we could only have one aircraft on the runway at a time. Once it was clear, the next one could come in, but the people in the watch office couldn't see with any accuracy where the first had got to, or whether it was moving well, and they had to wait until the pilot called "clear" before they gave the next man "pancake". And if the next man hadn't spaced himself out far enough, or the man in front took his time to clear the runway, or forgot to say so when he was clear, then number two would have to go round again, getting in everybody's way. When you're tired and hungry you tend to get impatient about delays, and that doesn't improve your flying, which is probably not at its best anyway.

Crummy and his Senior Air Traffic Control Officer put some thought into the problem, and came up with some good ideas. First, they borrowed a vertical searchlight from the AA unit at Grimsby, and put it just outside the perimeter track at the westward end of the long runway. It was a powerful beam, and you could see it through 2,000 feet of cloud. That made it a lot easier to orbit base without keeping the navigator at work. Then they double-banked the glim lamps for the last 200 yards of the runway, so that you needn't start slowing down until you reached them. Thirdly, they stationed a man with a field telephone halfway down the runway, with the job of telling control when the landing aircraft passed him. Then the controller could let the next man into the "funnels" position. These measures cut the interval between landings down to ninety seconds, for which we were duly grateful.

"Rear-gunner talking. There's an aircraft on the starboard quarter, high. I can't identify it, but it's overtaking us. Can you see it, mid-upper?"

"No, not yet. I'm looking — ah — got it! At four o'clock now, and catching us up. What the hell is it?"

I listened anxiously to their dialogue. Any faster aircraft was suspect as it could be a fighter. It might be a Mosquito, but the Mossie pilots knew the problems of identification, and usually gave us a wide berth.

"Mid-upper to skipper. Stand by to corkscrew starboard. He's at two o'clock now, slightly high. I can't . . ."

He was interrupted by the chatter of the front gulls, as Larry opened fire. I kicked the rudders to the right, and as we turned I saw with dismay that the double stream of .303 was accurately directed at the cabin of another Lancaster. I pulled the nose up hard, and the tracer bullets sprayed towards the stars.

"Cease fire, Larry, it's a Lanc."

When I levelled out, we searched the blackness for the other bomber, but it had vanished from our sight. Lanham broke the silence.

"Myring, you stupid, murdering bastard, the mid-upper had that aircraft under observation. You had no call to open fire."

"Aw — lay off, Charlie. Shoot first and ask questions afterwards, that's me, mate."

"I'm going to fix you, Myring. That might have been one of our own squadron. When we get down, you'd better not be there, or I'll have you."

"Ah — stop your whinging. I don't reckon it was a Lanc, anyway."

"Listen, Myring, you . . ."

I intervened.

"Shut up, the pair of you. We'll sort it out later. Right now, we've got two hours to go to the Dutch coast."

Walker and I were shutting down the engines, when Lanham appeared at the rear of the cabin, squeezing past the navigator's seat. His jaw was set, and he held the fire axe in his hand. He crouched on all fours and wriggled under Walker's seat. Remembering Larry and the gunner's threat, I flicked the mike switch on my mask.

"Get out quick, Larry, and run!"

I tried to get my right leg in Lanham's way, but only succeeded in kicking his arm as he crawled past below me. Fortunately, the impact of the heavy boot was enough to make him drop the axe. I held the mask aside, and shouted at him:

"Hey, you silly bastard, hold it!"

He wriggled and cursed. I pushed the boot into his back, and let it take my weight.

"Be your age, Charlie."

He looked up at me, and the glitter faded from his eyes.

"Okay, Jack, have it your way. But I'll report him at interrogation."

"I'll report him, if anyone does. Give me a hand with this gear."

I returned from a short leave to find a noisy crowd in the mess at nine o'clock in the evening. The Squadron Commander was banging a tankard on the table at the end of the ante-room, and calling for order. I shouldered my way in beside Jimmy, and asked him what was going on.

"They're auctioning Jacko's things. He bought it over Hanover while we were away."

A number of books and magazines were knocked down for a shilling, and a toilet case went for five bob. When a bicycle was wheeled forward, one of the "B" flight pilots stood up.

"I claim that lot, sir. It was promised to me by the owner."

"Right," said the Squadron Commander, "any witnesses?"

The claimant's navigator put up a hand.

"Yes, it's right enough, sir. My skipper often used to borrow that bike, and Jacko sort of bequeathed it to him."

"In what way?"

"Well, he said: 'If I ever get the chop, you can have the old bike, you bludger.'"

We laughed at that, and the Squadron Commander said:

"Good enough, I'll accept that as a genuine bequest. It's yours, Joe, take it away."

The adjutant leaned forward, and spoke quietly to the pilot. He nodded and stood up again.

"I'll put the bike back in the auction, sir."

There was a mumble of approval.

"Well done, Joe. Right, I'm putting this excellent machine up, gentlemen, now what am I bid? Come along, do I hear ten shillings to start? I'm told it is perfectly roadworthy . . ."

Someone called out, "Demonstration!" which we all took up, until Joe mounted the bicycle and performed a few unsteady figures of eight on the carpet. The Squadron Commander raised his voice above the applause.

"Come along now, gentlemen, let me have a bid. All proceeds to the next of kin. Do I hear seven-and-six?"

Eventually Joe succeeded in retaining his promised bicycle at a cost of twenty-five shillings, and the auction went on. Hilarity increased, and bidding became more adventurous, as thirsts were assuaged. I had spent my last few shillings on the taxi fare from Lincoln station, and couldn't even buy myself a beer.

On outings to Lincoln, or on leave journeys to and from the railway station, we patronised Kirk's Taxi Service. Somehow, the aged Austin limousine and its proprietor contrived to meet our needs by day or night. The taxi held the whole crew at a pinch, and it was a practicable luxury when shared between us for a shilling a mile.

Mr Kirk was short and spherically shaped. He elevated his head, which was totally bald, to the required line of sight for driving by seating himself on three fat cushions. From this commanding position, he drove with the utmost caution and, in my experience, never exceeded a speed of thirty miles an hour. He soon knew the crew by their first names, but so venerable was his appearance, and so dignified his bearing, that we could never bring ourselves to address him other than as Mr Kirk. He was an inveterate philosophiser, and seemed to take it as his duty to meet our every problem with an unbroken front of wisdom and advice. He dispensed guidance and counsel whilst he drove, like a travelling oracle.

At Christmas, he entertained us to the best meal that Lincoln could provide, followed by a box at the Theatre Royal for the pantomime. He detailed one of his sons to drive the taxi, the better himself to concentrate upon his duties as a host.

It was always comforting to recognise his bald head, gleaming in the station ticket office, on emerging from the noisome London train, and I found it very easeful to sit back, bathed in the stream of his philosophising, as we motored gently up the Wragby road to Wickenby.

Another rubicund and balding character (although in his case the loss of hair was premature) was the navigator Leo Oldmixon. We had got used to seeing him around as a flight sergeant in the Royal Canadian Air Force, although we knew he was an American by

178

birth. One lunchtime, however, he appeared in the officers' mess wearing the uniform of a second lieutenant in the United States Army Air Force. I had to look closely at the chubby, moustached face before I recognised him. We offered congratulations on his promotion, and on his translation.

"Congrats, old boy. Welcome to the mess."

"Good on you, Leo. Canuck one day, Yank the next!"

"Revealed in your true colours at last, eh?"

"Just look at that uniform. What quality!"

Oldmixon pushed a hand into the pocket of the smooth, beige slacks.

"Thank you, gentlemen. I believe I may buy a round of drinks on this occasion."

The Station Commander turned from the bar.

"You must have your first drink in the mess with me, Oldmixon. What will it be?"

"Well, sir, you're a group captain and I'm only a second looey, but I figure our pay's about the same. What d'you say we toss for it?"

Watson turned to me, his hoarse whisper echoed in my ear.

"Stone me, does he really get as much as the old man?"

"I shouldn't be surprised."

"We're in the wrong air force, mate. Er — mine's a bitter, lieutenant."

Of the many routes we took to Germany, I preferred those leading to the southern targets, for then there was no need to climb in dreary circles over base; we could gain height as we travelled south to Selsey Bill or Beachy Head, above the darkened but familiar English countryside, and across the narrow Channel into France. Although the German gunners in their French emplacements bombarded us in transit, we knew that in the farms and villages below were friendly hands to help the fallen airman, and secret ways that led to neutral lands.

I liked less the eastward route from Mablethorpe, across the grey North Sea to the Ruhr. The Dutch coast flashed, and not only with gunfire, but with the rippling, white-hot bursts which could be nothing else but British bombs. It was hard to understand what lay behind these premature releases. Some were presumably due to technical malfunctions which forced the crews to turn for home, dropping their bombs off on the way. But whole bomb loads being jettisoned wouldn't make those single flashes; they looked more to me like cookies, as though the captain was throwing his biggest bomb away before flying into enemy territory. The only reason for such an action would be to gain more altitude. I could understand that it wasn't any fun to bomb a target in the Ruhr from 14,000 or 15,000 feet, as some of the older bombers did, when the rest of us were up at 20,000. There would be more hardware falling from above than coming upwards from the guns. Nevertheless, it seemed a humiliating and wasteful thing to do and, sitting in the comparatively high-flying Lancaster, I could afford to be censorious.

Not that the Lancaster would always climb as well as I wanted her to, certainly not on warm nights. In accordance with some law of physics, which I didn't fully understand, the colder the air the better she went up. Crummy once sent someone up to try to set a record, and he got to well over 27,000 feet, fully laden, but I never reached much above 24,000 in a Lancaster, and that was on the way home with the bombs gone. Reaching 20,000 feet before the Ruhr was difficult enough, but it was trying to rise above high cloud *en route* that gave me the creeps. Driven, not by any tactical reason, but by some psychophysical impulse, I fought to claw my way into the clear. It was sometimes like being in that dream when you can't breathe, and your brain sends your muscles panic signals to get your nose out of the pillow, or when at the seaside you dive deeper under a wave than you intended and must kick hard to reach the surface before your breath runs out. The cloud muffled the strong sound of the engines, as though they too were short of breath. It reflected the exhaust flames in a dull red haze. There was no sense of forward movement, as though the aircraft were a ship that lay at anchor in a fog.

I sought to believe the instruments in front of me: the ASI, altimeter, artificial horizon, the indicators of vertical speed and turn and slip. But I still sneaked upward glances through the canopy, searching for the hard indigo of open sky, or the flat white pinpoint of a star. I set up a gentle switchback motion, down and up, down and up, then tried to hold the few feet we gained at the top of the upswing. I put a little flap down; the altered airflow lifted us momentarily. I tried to milk off the flap so gently that the aircraft didn't notice. By such manoeuvres, we might gain 100 feet or so for fifteen minutes' work. The cloud still wrapped about us as closely as before. Craving a victim for my spleen, I thought of the meteorologist, back on the ground at Wickenby.

"Jim, I thought that bloody met man said cloud tops 16,000."

"That's right."

"Well, he ought to pull his finger out. We're at 19,000 and still in ten-tenths lag. Bloody man."

"Yeah, well, he did say layers of alto-stratus above."

"Eh? I never heard him say that."

"He did, Jack. I wrote it down in the log."

"Oh. Anyway, he's still wrong. It's not layered, it's solid."

The navigator was clearly agog with indifference. How do you like that, Jimmy siding with the met man? What else can you expect? They don't appreciate a pilot's problems. I'd like to see them keeping this thing steady for hours on instruments.

Paranoia slowly conquered claustrophobia, and in turn gave way to rationality. I put the stars out of my mind, settled more comfortably in the seat, and pretended that I was in the Link Trainer for an hour or two. It became quite tolerable after a while, but it was still a wonderful relief when the cloud began to thin out, showed glimpses of the sky, and drew back like a veil while we emerged, high and free, into the vast expanse of night. Suddenly the cabin was a warm, familiar place, the oxygen smelt cleaner and the instrument panel no longer filled my world.

So I occupied the time *en route* to central Germany, while Cassidy juggled with the G-box, Fairbairn tuned in to the half-hour broadcasts, Myring peered blindly through the perspex in the nose, and Walker watched the gauges. The waiting gunners in the turrets must have found the time passed slowly, and even more so on the long sea-crossing to attack the northern targets, for those three hundred and sixty miles from Lincolnshire to Denmark seemed an eternity of nothing. It happened that we were on leave when the Command took that dreary route again to bomb Berlin. It was a punishing operation for our colleagues in 460 Squadron in Binbrook, who lost five crews that night.

We flew fighter-affiliation exercises with the Spitfires from Kirton-in-Lindsey on 10 and 11 December. Both times we took along one of the newly arrived pilots, to whom I was required to demonstrate the standard techniques of evasive action. When the fighter pilots pressed their triggers they shot not cannon shells but photographs, and we did our best to make their aim as difficult as possible. There was an element of fun in the mock combats and, indeed, our call sign for the fighter was always "Playmate", but the practice helped to hone the edge of our reactions, and the exercise was good for my arm and leg muscles. Later, when the photographs had been developed and their purport analysed, our playmates would fly to Wickenby to gloat over us with the evidence of gun sights full of Lancaster, at which our gunners would make derisive noises, saying, "We'd have blown you out of the sky before you ever got that shot in!" But we knew that the fighter's guns out ranged our 303s by far, and that, by day at least, all the advantage lay with them.

The big city was again the target on 16 December when we set off in Charlie Two on a seven-hour mission. Sergeant Elkington, another new arrival, came along as second-dicky, but he gained little experience from the trip as we flew in almost continuous cloud, so deep and thick that Wing Commander Leonard Cheshire, acting as master bomber, could find no way to mark the target for the PFF to light. I took advantage of Elkington's presence to take some respite from sitting at the wheel. I put him in the left-hand seat on the way home from Berlin, told him to keep at 20,000 feet and steer whatever courses the navigator told him, and to call me if anything horrible happened. Then I toured the aircraft from nose to tail, playing the fool. When Myring raised his eyebrows at my appearance by his side, I pretended that I was trying to find my parachute; with a view to bailing out. Back at the main spar, I shouted the information into Fairbairn's ear that I was a staff officer from the Air Ministry, conducting a survey into the question of aircrew morale. Clutching one of Protheroe's booted legs in the mid-upper turret, I pantomimed a drunkard looking for the Elsan with little time to spare. Little Derek Elkington must have impressed me as a good, reliable pilot for me to have behaved so; goodness knows what he must have thought of me.

Four hundred and ninety-two aircraft were dispatched on this mission, and of these 450 reached Berlin.

Twenty-five failed to return to England, and fog lying thickly on East Anglia took a dreadful toll of those who did get back. A further twenty-nine bombers crashed while groping blindly for their bases in the murk, as we passed above them on our careful way to Wickenby.

The flight office was small and sparsely furnished. When the windows were closed, it soon became intolerably stuffy as the odour of human beings, the smell of tobacco and the coke fumes from the stove mingled noxiously together. Opening the windows lowered the temperature drastically, and encouraged the fumes to ignore the stovepipe entirely, in favour of the room. We chose slow suffocation, in some degree of warmth, in preference to quick asphyxiation in the cold. Yellowing upon the walls clung vast, complex diagrams depicting Lancasters in such states of undress as might best reveal the convolutions of their fuel and hydraulic systems. A well thumbed copy of "Tee Emm" and some less handled issues of "Aircraft Recognition" lay on trestle tables. We hadn't been flying the previous night, and I came into the office shortly after nine o'clock, earlier than usual, to secure a seat in one of the dilapidated armchairs. Conversation was desultory and, as usual, ninety-nine per cent shop.

"The under cart was jammed; I had to make a belly-landing on the grass."

"Shaky do, eh? Did you try the emergency air?"

"No, I didn't. I thought there might be a flak hole in the pipe and I'd p'raps finish up with one wheel locked down and the other not . . ."

"Actually, it's quite fun landing on one wheel."

"I'll take your word for it. Anyway, I got the crew to ditching stations, strapped myself in tight, and put her down alongside the short runway. Piece of cake."

"Much damage?"

"Not bad, really. Of course, the props are a bit bent, and the bomb-doors got pretty well scraped, but they reckon it can all be repaired on the unit."

"Good show. Where did you get hit?"

"I think it must've been Texel. They had a go at us there, and I heard a few pings on the old fuselage."

"You shouldn't have been over Texel."

"All right, ace. We were a bit south of track, that's all."

"Could happen to anyone."

"Another new crew bought it, I see."

"Yes, I noticed we'd moved up one on the leave roster. Who was it?"

"Don't know. Scots name — Mac something."

"Have you seen what's on at the station cinema?"

"Saw it in Lincoln. Paulette Goddard's in it. She's a smasher."

"Too right. Well, I've got an air test on Charlie Two. I'll be seeing you."

"Keep your finger out."

With no bomb load to carry, and her fuel tanks half empty for the air test, Charlie Two jumped off the runway like a startled rabbit. I held the nose down until the speed built up to 150, and then pulled her into a steep, climbing turn to port, that pressed our bottoms hard into our seats. As the horizon tilted down the sky, I chanted:

"In mah P40 pursoot ship, with an itsy-bitsy take-off, Ah hit the air. And Ah climbed: twenny thousan' feet, thirdy thousan' feet, fordy thousan' feet . . ."

Still winding on the turn, I shoved the nose down sharply, to point at the centre of the airfield.

". . . an' there Ah put mah P40 pursoot ship into a dive: three hunnerd miles per hour, four hunnerd miles per hour, five hunnerd miles per hour. An' then the tail assembly broke off. What did Ah do? Man, Ah hit the silk . . ."

Cassidy spoke patiently, but I thought I detected a hint of edginess in his voice:

"D'you reckon you could hold her straight and level for a few minutes, Jack? I am supposed to check the G-box."

My spirits stayed high while we checked that all the bits of Charlie Two were working well, but they fell a little when we walked into the briefing room that evening, and saw the mission that was planned for us. On some previous operations, the German fighters had been drawn away from us by other bombers making spoof attacks. Now, on 20 December, it was Wickenby's turn to provide the diversionary effort. We were to fly straight for Mannheim as the decoys, while the rest of the Command turned northwards to make the main assault on Frankfurt.

The Rhine was easily identified as we approached, and the target was visible through scattered wisps of cloud. I had expected, indeed feared, to attract some

187

massive opposition in that clear winter night, but we sailed on unscathed, as in a dream, across Mannheim through a passive searchlight belt. When the bombs had gone, we turned to join the mainstream's homeward route and, passing north of fireswept Frankfurt, we watched with sympathy as low-flying Halifaxes were picked off by accurate bursts of heavy flak. Our feeling for the victims was, as ever, not unmingled with a half-acknowledged sense of relief that our lot was not theirs. Just as an ageing uncle of mine would read the obituary columns in the newspaper, saying, "I wonder whether anyone I know has given up smoking today," and smiling grimly to find a familiar name, not because the man's demise had pleased him, but simply savouring his own survival.

The operation, which took us less than six hours to fly, cost the Command forty-four bombers. It was important to us for another reason: it was Charlie Lanham's last. He had flown twenty-one missions with us, and these, when added to those he had previously done in Wellingtons, gave him a total of thirty operations and a completed tour. I nourished an unspoken hope that he might elect to stay and fly with us until the end of our tour, and I had the impression that Protheroe, with whom his personal and tactical understanding had been close, shared that hope. But another six operations, most of which were likely to be on the German capital, were more than comradeship could ask, particularly of a man who had been away from his home, 12,000 miles away, for two and a half years. Whether the thought occurred to Lanham I didn't know, but he made no sign, and we marked his leaving with revelry that held some element of sorrow.

Balancing on the balls of his feet, dapper and shining in his best blue uniform, the rear-gunner shook my hand.

"Good luck, Jack. Keep away from the grog, and you'll be okay. Take care of them, George — it's up to you now."

Christmas came, and I was hypocritically shocked to find that the squadron was on call for operations. Indeed, a general lack of enthusiasm was apparent in the flight office.

"Ops on Christmas Day, I reckon that's a poor show."

Yeah, it doesn't seem right, does it?"

"In the first war, the chaps in the front line had a sort of unofficial truce. They played soccer, and swopped hats. Handed fags round and all that."

"We ought to refuse to fly."

In the event, we were stood down by midday, and we too had a football match. 626 Squadron beat 12 Squadron for a cup, presented by the Station Commander. It was a revelation to see the groundcrew airmen, known to us as muffed figures, anonymously crouched or clambering about our aircraft, suddenly transformed, and showing speed and skill as they leaped and sprinted in the muddied goalmouths.

CHAPTER EIGHT

1944 and the Big Black Beaut

On the first day of 1944, the target for an all-Lancaster attack was yet again Berlin. The aircraft was our customary Charlie Two, but the crew had suffered changes. Lanham had gone, and in his rear-turret seat was Len Bretell, a cool, experienced gunner, nearing the end of his second operational tour. Young George Wilson deputised for Larry Myring, who was absent on commissioning leave. Never again was I to write in my logbook: "Crew as before." There were new names alongside mine on the battle order, fresh faces beside me in the briefing room, strange voices on the intercom.

An obstruction on the taxiway caused a delay at take-off time, and many pilots found their engines over-heating as they waited in the darkness. Seven of them were forced to shut down, and missed the take-off deadline. By turning a blind eye to the mounting temperature gauges, we contrived to get into the air thirty-four minutes after midnight, just within the permitted time.

190

For Cassidy and me, this was our twenty-fourth operational flight together, and our conversation in the air, through usage, had become abbreviated to the point of cryptology. Chief among the reasons for our brevity was the fact that I was never to miss the gunner's first call of "fighter", because of some long-winded passage between other members of the crew. Brevity was fine, but now we fell into a self-laid trap. A little more than half-way to the target, we were flying at 150mph, on an easterly heading, when the navigator spoke:

"Nav to pilot. Make it 155."

Dimly my semi-somnolent brain registered the message; it had the normal word form for a change of course. Requests for alterations in airspeed were usually couched in an interrogative form. Nevertheless, this was an abnormally large change of heading, so I checked with Cassidy.

"155?"

"Yes, 155."

Still neither of us mentioned degrees or mph. I swung Charlie Two into a steady starboard turn, until the compass ticked round on to 155 degrees. Ten minutes later, we were being warmly received by the defences of some large city, where no large city should have been. I told the navigator:

"We're over a heavily defended area, Jimmy, and I don't see any other aircraft around. Any ideas?"

"Cripes, Jack, I don't know. It can only be Hanover, but we're way off track if it is. Wait a sec — there should be some green route markers going down about now. Can you see any sign of them?"

"Stand by."

The flight engineer and I searched as much of the night as we could see, without result, then Protheroe called.

"Mid-upper to skipper. Green flares on the port quarter, a long way off."

The navigator's voice was sharp with anxiety.

"I heard that, Jack. How far away are the flares, mid-upper? Can you make a guess?"

"It's hard to tell. I should think thirty or forty miles away, Jim."

"Oh, cripes. You probably are over Hanover, Jack. You'd better alter course on to 045 degrees, while I figure out a new course for the target. Gee, there must have been a complete change of wind, or . . ."

But the truth was dawning on me now.

"Jimmy, you know that big alteration of course you gave me, about ten minutes ago . . ."

"What change of course? What are you steering?"

"155 — like you said."

"Oh, no! That was airspeed. Gosh, Jack, I'm sorry. I should've said mph . . ."

"My fault, nav. I should have checked it properly. Let's have some revs, Johnny."

Charlie Two shook in protest, as we applied climbing power in level flight, and hastened in pursuit of the bomber stream. In due course, and duly chastened, we brought up the rear over Berlin, where pools of flaming phosphorous lit the city streets, and vast, unheard explosions rent the night.

There was a light covering of snow on the runway when we landed at 7.15 in the morning of 2 January, and it was falling thickly by the time we had run the engines down in dispersal. We waited in the piercing cold, cowering under Charlie Two's great wings, until the crew bus came whining through the snowflakes to take us to interrogation. The Church of England padre stood beaming at the hatchway in the entrance to the briefing room, dispensing cocoa, cigarettes and rum. For once I took a mouthful of the spirit before taking my place among the crew at one of the debriefing tables. As we described the salient features of the mission to the WAAF intelligence officer, whose platinum hair gleamed as she bent over the report form, I could taste the rum-fumes on my palate.

The crew slumped uncomfortably in the slatted folding chairs, their facial muscles slackening, showing grimy shadows where the oxygen masks had rubbed against the skin. Cassidy's eyes were strained, his forehead furrowed, as he sat with shoulders hunched, reading from his log the positions at which we had sighted such phenomena as fighter flares, aircraft shot down and lights on the ground. I turned away from his recital to see which other crews were present and which were yet to come. I missed Lanham's presence, and his personality, which could be trusted to enliven even such an anti-climactic scene as this. His successor sat, composed and silent, a cigarette held steadily between

193

his lips, hands folded in his lap. Clearly, Bretell would be no second Lanham; there would be no leg-pulling and no chuckles. But his serenity was not displeasing. Walker's fair hair was dishevelled and he looked dispirited, his eyes a vacant blue, blinking involuntarily in the harsh electric light. Fairbairn's long chin showed an early morning stubble and, as he waited patiently to speak his piece, his fingers constantly pushed a strand of hair back from his forehead. Protheroe sat with Bretell, smoking a free-issue cigarette, with another stuck behind his ear. He was the youngest of us and, although his face was sallow and begrimed, his eyes were bright and he winked cheerfully when he caught my glance.

At length, the lady let us go and another crew took our places at her table. Outside, the snow had reached the deep and crisp and even stage. We stumbled through it to our messes, bolted down the breakfast and crept into our chilly beds at half past eight. Before I fell asleep, the searchlight beams and gun flashes of the night flickered inside my eyelids, and the roar of Merlin engines still echoed in my head. I could taste the oxygen, and traces of the rum. At least, I thought, with all that snow there'll be no ops tonight. Lovely snow, fall thick and fast, bury the airfield and all the Lancasters, lovely, lovely snow.

At three o'clock in the afternoon, I woke when the door flew open and a cheerful early riser strode into the hut.

"Wakey, wakey, rise and shine! Ops again tonight, you lucky people. Show a leg!"

I could just move my lips enough to whimper:

"What about the snow?"

"All being nicely cleared away. The Old Man's got every non-aircrew bod out on the runway with a spade, himself and all the chairborne types as well. They've got to do five yards each or die. Jolly good show, isn't it?"

I lay in a warm, foetal huddle in the bed, but my soul had turned to ice. My ears were still ringing, I could still taste rum, and I cursed Group Captain Crummy, his spades, and all his works.

By the evening of Sunday 2 January, the Station Commander and his labour gang, with assistance from the Sno-Go sweeper, had cleared the main runway. They hadn't been able to clear the snow from the Drem lighting, so they had put out gooseneck flares instead. At 11.30 we were airborne again in Charlie Two, one of about 400 aircraft detailed to attack Berlin. At briefing the IO had said, with a smile:

"Reports indicate that the city's anti-aircraft guns are now being fired by fifteen-year-old boys of the Hitler Youth Movement as fast as Russian POWs can load them."

We had responded with an automatic guffaw, but I didn't really find the remark amusing; the cold statistics of the previous night's attack were that 421 aircraft set out, 386 reached the target, and 28 were lost. No doubt, the demands of the eastern front had drawn off the cream of the flak gunners, and it was the rapid expansion of the night-fighter force that accounted for our mounting losses, but the radar-predicted gunfire still had a salutary effect. I, for one, never found it comical.

We had John Colles at the radio in place of Charlie Fairbairn, who was in bed with a bad cold, and another stand-in bomb-aimer. Colles usually flew with Warrant Officer Smith, and I knew him to be a capable wireless-operator. He was a massive young man, well-spoken, with an unusual courtesy in his manner, and a strongly boned face under a shock of dark curls. On this occasion, he was to have his full share of the action. While we were still climbing over base, before setting course with the first wave, he picked up a W/T broadcast on the Group operational frequency, recalling us from the mission, and directing us to land at Exeter. We had never received a general recall message before, but I was aware that such an action could happen in certain circumstances, for example in the event of a sudden deterioration in the weather. However, something made me suspicious of the instruction, and I couldn't accept it at face value.

"You're sure it's for us, John?"

"Yes, captain, it's correctly prefixed with the Group call sign."

"And then?"

" 'Immediate recall. Land at Exeter.' And a date-time group."

It didn't make sense. I made a slow, careful search of the sky: some thin cirrus, patches of alto-cumulus, nothing in the least menacing. And how could we all possibly land at Exeter?

"The weather looks all right to me. We'll press on and wait for a repeat."

"Very well, captain."

An hour later, when we were half-way across the North Sea, Colles reported again.

"Wireless-operator to captain. You were right; I've just had a cancellation of the recall. We're to continue as briefed."

It transpired that the original broadcast was intended for a small force of Wellingtons, who were being kept out of our way. But the damage had already been partially done; 113 of our aircraft aborted, and landed at Exeter. The Control Officer there must have wondered whether he were the victim of a practical joke on a very large scale.

We reached Berlin on time, and received a warm welcome from the fifteen-year-olds, and their POW assistants. It seemed to me that the flak was, if anything, more intense and accurate than ever, and I swore at the memory of the IO's joke.

Bretell called me from the rear-turret and, for once, his voice betrayed some agitation.

"I don't think I'm getting oxygen, skipper. I can't feel any coming through the tube, and I'm getting a bit dizzy."

"Stand by, Len. Wireless-op, will you go down and check the rear-gunner's tube? Take a portable bottle with you, okay?"

"Yes, captain, going off intercom now."

Now the new bomb-aimer, who had come to the squadron after many months on instructional duties in

Training Command, made his contribution to the unhappy mission. At his request, I had opened the bomb-doors some minutes previously, and flown grimly straight and level through the heavy flak, hoping that at any second he would drop the bombs, and let me close the doors, and get away from there. He had other ideas.

"Bomb-aimer to pilot. Are you ready to commence the bombing-run?"

"Ready? I've been ready and waiting for the last ten minutes!"

"Thank you, pilot. I am satisfied that the bomb-sight is levelled, and all stations selected."

"Get cracking, then."

"Thank you, pilot. Commencing bombing run now. Right . . . steady. Right . . . steady. Left, left . . . steady. Right a bit . . . steady."

My God, I thought, it's really going to happen, he's going to say "back a bit". But there was worse to come:

"Right . . . steady. Right . . . steady. Right . . . right . . . dummy run!"

I sensed, rather than saw, the flight engineer stiffen in horror beside me. I spoke as calmly as I could.

"You don't do dummy runs on Berlin. Let 'em go."

"But . . ."

"Let 'em go."

I felt Charlie Two lift as the high explosives tumbled out of the bomb-bay, and my heart lifted with her. Later, I would explain to our new colleague the essential differences in technique between bombing the Big City, and bombing practise ranges in the Midlands. I had no scruples about accepting the bombing-error; I knew well enough that this was no precision target, to be hit with pinpoint accuracy.

Colles called from the intercom plug at the rear door. His voice sounded even, and good-humoured.

"I think the rear-gunner is semi-conscious, captain. His oxygen tube must have frozen up — I can feel the ice in it — and the heating for his suit may have failed; he seems awfully cold."

"You can reach him?"

"Oh, yes."

"Can you get him out of the turret, and get in yourself?"

"I will if I can, captain."

The rear-gunner's predicament was worrying without heat or oxygen he was unlikely to survive the mission, if I continued to fly at 20,000 feet in temperatures of thirty degrees or more below zero. I was reminded of the Hagen operation on 1 October, when a shell fragment had punctured Lanham's oxygen tube. On that occasion, I had revived the rear-gunner by flying at a lower level, but then most of the homeward route had been over France. This time we were deep within the heart of Germany, nearly 400 miles from the Dutch coast. It would be a perilous passage for a low-flying aircraft, but clearly I couldn't let Bretell die of cold and lack of oxygen.

Colles's calm voice sounded again in my head-phones.

"I'm afraid I can't persuade the rear-gunner to leave his turret."

"Don't persuade him, John. Just drag him out."

"That's what I tried to do, captain, but he wouldn't come. He fought with me, quite strongly."

"He's conscious, then?"

"On and off. He seems to wake up when I touch him."

This was a snag; Bretell's sense of duty was working to our disadvantage. His instinct to stay at his post was strong, and unaffected by the fact that, half-conscious, he was useless there. I wanted him wrapped up on the rest-bed while Colles, a trained gunner, manned his turret.

"Look, John, you're going to have to get rough. You're big and he's little. Sock him if you have to, but get him out."

"Very well, captain. I'll have to come back and get another oxygen bottle — this one's running out."

"Roger."

We were circumnavigating Hanover when the next excitement happened. The "Boozer" warning light on the instrument panel flashed on, telling me that Charlie Two was being plotted by the enemy radar. I told George Protheroe to keep an even stricter look-out than usual, but as the radar-directed fighters' approach was usually from below the stern, the view that mattered was the rear-gunner's. I rolled the wings through sixty degrees each way, to give the mid-upper a fair chance of examining the danger area. He reported that a succession of fighter flares was being dropped astern of us, at about 2,000 yards range. I didn't like the sound of that, and put the aircraft into a standard corkscrew pattern. Colles came through on the intercom again.

"I'm very sorry, captain. The rear-gunner insists on staying in the turret. He's really very determined, and I can't get enough leverage to pull him out, or enough room to knock him out. Also, he's hit me so often in the face with his elbow, that I can't quite see what I'm doing. I'm awfully sorry."

"Okay, John, you've done your best. Scrub it, and get back to your set."

The "Boozer" light still flashed, and the prolonged evasive manoeuvres were carrying us far south of track, away from the main stream. This was just as well if the radar was using Charlie Two as a guide, for the fighters would hunt in vain behind us for their victims. I returned to my thoughts about Bretell; if he were strong enough to fight off so powerful a man as Colles, he couldn't be entirely without oxygen. It seemed probable that some was finding a way through to him along the ice-bound tube. I resolved to remain at the briefed altitude, until we were within fifty miles of the Dutch coast, and then to commence a slow descent.

This we did, and, although we continued to receive the "Boozer" warnings, the mid-upper gunner never saw a fighter all the way. He was near to tears with exhaustion and frustration by the time we crossed the coastline.

The weather was rapidly deteriorating, and when we reached the area of Wickenby, conditions were very poor. Control suggested that we divert to Acklington, 170 miles away, north of Newcastle. But we had been in the air for seven hours, and Bretell was stiff with cold, so I demurred:

"Darky from Charlie Two. I have a casualty on board. Request permission to try landing, over."

"Charlie Two, stand by."

A moment passed, and I peered through the thickening gloom, trying to keep the scanty aerodrome lights in sight, as we banked around the circuit.

"Charlie Two, this is Darky, over?"

"Darky, go ahead."

"Charlie Two, you have permission to attempt one, repeat one, landing. Exercise caution. What is the nature of your casualty, over?"

"Rear-gunner, cold and anoxia. Possible frostbite, over."

"Roger, Charlie Two. Ambulance will be standing by. Out."

We made a low, tight circuit and, as I lowered the wheels, I noticed that the bomb-aimer was crawling under Walker's seat. He struggled to his feet, behind the engineer, and plugged into the intercom. I was surprised.

"What's the matter, bomb-aimer?"

"Nothing, pilot. Standing orders are that the bomb-aimer should vacate the nose compartment before landing."

I shrugged, and wondered whether Myring had ever heard of that standing order. Walker banged the full flap down, and I let Charlie Two fall fast. I pulled the nose up, as we came through the threshold lights, and gave her a little burst of motor. She floated, floated, down the runway, as I held the wheel hard back. I felt the tension in my muscles, felt the sweat start on my flesh.

"Get down, you big, black bastard."

She touched the concrete with a whisper, not a bounce. Cassidy's voice was admonitory:

"Take it back, Jack. She's not a bastard, she's a beauty."

"Sorry, Charlie Two, I unsay that remark. You are a big, black beauty."

Rory was a mid-upper gunner, neat and well groomed, with a face like that of a contented cat. He spoke with a lisp and a lilting, feminine diction, and he used scented soaps and lotions. He occasionally dabbed his nose with a small, silk handkerchief. However, he was well advanced on his second tour of operations, and he wore a DFM ribbon and a wound stripe, so his manner escaped the abuse which it might have otherwise attracted, in the aggressively masculine society in which he moved. One evening, at the bar in the officers' mess, he was describing the glories of his West End flat.

"Lovely fitted carpets up to your ankles, dear, and such beautiful pictures on the walls. And I had these wonderful pieces of sculpture, done in Scandinavian wood by this marvellous Polish person . . ."

In the group round Rory were several robust Australians, whose aesthetic interests it would not be too harsh to term philistine, embracing as they did little beyond the world of sport and "Sheilas". I could tell that they regarded Rory's little world of cultivated comfort with some derision, but they urged him to continue his tale.

"Well, in the dreadful blitz, there was this absolute disaster, when a horrid bomb came right through the ceiling into my lovely living-room."

There was a chorus of mock disbelief and protest at the outrage, but Rory was undeterred. His voice became shrill with indignation.

"My dears, it wasn't so much the dreadful damage that the bomb did, it was the absolute havoc caused by the fire brigade. I can't tell you what a mess they made. All my lovely pictures were just soggy scraps of paint and canvas and, as for my books, the priceless first editions that I'd collected over the years . . . and the busts . . ."

This time the interruptions were hilarious and prolonged.

"Oh no, not the beaut busts, Rory!"

"Jeez, what a bloody awful crime!"

"Wouldn't it give you the horrors?"

"A man would have to be a proper bastard to bust Rory's busts, though, wouldn't he?"

Under normal circumstances, I would have expected Rory to subside into a fit of giggles at the sallies, but he stood very still while his face grew pink and tears filled his eyes. Then he flung himself at his nearest listener, flailing at the broad, mocking face with fragile fists. The tall Australian was taken aback and retreated behind an even larger colleague, who caught the little gunner's wrists and held them firmly.

"Steady on, Rory, old feller, no harm meant."

But Rory's blood was up, and he fought to free himself from the restraining grasp.

"You dare to sneer at my precious things, you ignorant colonial. How could you understand anything about art or beauty? All you know or care about are rabbits, and sheep, and . . . and kangaroos! You only came over here as an excuse to get away from your own awful, uncultured country . . ."

"Yeah, that's right, Rory mate, good on you. Let's have a grog on it, what d'you say?"

The tide of Rory's temper ebbed as quickly as it had flowed. He smoothed his hair, and gave a twinkling smile.

"Thanks very much. I'll have a gin and lime, if it's all the same to you."

There were fewer of us in the mess than usual to witness Rory's outburst, because the squadron's crews were widely dispersed after the Berlin operation of 2 January. Only the Australians Hutchinson and Wellham, Warrant Officer Rew and I had landed at Wickenby, four pilots had obeyed the spurious recall message and were packed on Exeter airfield like sardines in a tin; the remaining six had been diverted to the far north east of England. But thirteen crews had reassembled by Wednesday 5 January, and were ordered to attack Stettin. Of these, two failed to leave the ground because of technical snags, and we set off in Charlie Two at ten minutes to midnight for what was to be the longest sortie of the tour.

We crossed the English coast outbound at Mablethorpe and turned north-east, still climbing, on our course for

Denmark. There we headed east across the mainland and the Kattegat, north of Copenhagen, and over the lamplit towns of Sweden, to cross the Baltic Sea. Four hours after leaving base we passed over Rugen Island, west of Peenemunde, and turned south-east for Stettin.

The target lay, snow-covered, on the west bank of the river Oder in full moonlight. It was further lighted through a drifting veil of broken stratus, by incendiaries, marker flares and the prodigious flashes of the heavy bombs. As Charlie Two approached, the gunners of the port joined in, casting a resection in the sky around us of the pyrotechnic brilliance below. They threw up salvoes of brightly coloured tracer bullets and rockets which burst with startling radiance, while steeply tilted naval guns fired monstrous shells to towering, harmless heights above us.

Simultaneously, a well-timed spoof attack was being delivered on Berlin to draw the waiting fighter groups away from us, and we made the bombing run unchallenged from the air. Bluey Turner, who in November had flown with us to Düsseldorf, was once again the absent Myring's deputy. In welcome contrast to his studious predecessor at our bomb-sight, he delayed the opening of the bomb-doors so long as to let the falling "cookie" knock them wider as they spread. The load fell on a cluster of green target-indicators shimmering below.

Charlie Two droned on across the city, where the blaze of light, reflecting from the snow and from the river, struck more reflections from the perspex windows of the cockpit. Only the northern lights were needed to complete the spectacle of gaudy fantasy. Even the cloud seemed to be burning as we left the target and headed back above the Baltic. It glowed behind us still when we made a pinpoint on the southern tip of Bornholm, and turned north-west to join our outbound route.

When we were two hundred miles away from the English coast, Charlie Two was sleep-walking along the sky, barely acknowledging my gentle guidance to maintain our height and course, the waking sun lifted his head above the eastern cloud sheets and smiled at us across the depths of space. The sight brought back to me a line of Omar's Rubaiyat:

"Dreaming when Dawn's left hand was in the sky . . ."

Cassidy showed his appreciation of the allusion with a giggle, and continued the stanza:

"I heard a voice within the tavern cry
Awake, my little ones, and fill the cup,
Before life's liquor in its cup be dry . . ."

Walker suited the action to the words by pouring the last of the coffee into the cap of the thermos flask, and passing it to me. But it was still a long way to the nearest tavern, and Charlie Two seemed to go slower and slower as the dawn progressed.

The tavern must have seemed particularly distant to Noel Belford and his crew from Wickenby. Nobody knew exactly how to put a Lancaster down with safety on the water, especially not on a North Sea swell, which looked and hit the fuselage like corrugated iron. All you could do was learn the ditching drill, and trust to luck. Noel and his men had learned their drill, and their efforts were rewarded when Noel set his wounded aircraft down, somewhere beneath us, and it floated long enough for each man to get out. Everything worked according to the textbook: the navigator calculated their position, the wireless operator transmitted it, the dinghy inflated correctly, the crew broke through the hatches and embarked.

All that remained for them to do was wait, and try to keep warm and dry enough to stay alive until salvation came. This they did, huddled in the sickeningly rocking dinghy, watching the western horizon for sixteen freezing hours. They didn't wait in vain. By courtesy of a Royal Navy motor torpedo boat, Wickenby saw them back next day.

Now came the tune for Charlie Two's last operation. The ageing aircraft's fighting life was at an end, and she was to be put out to stud at a Lancaster training unit. We regretted that her time could not be extended, so that we might fly two more operations with her to end our tour. It was hard to believe that I would stress her more in action over Germany than she would suffer pounding round an airfield circuit, with a heavy-handed learner at the wheel. But our sentiments weighed little against the ponderous regulations. Len Bretell's case made a human parallel to that of Charlie Two, but since he could speak up for himself, it had a different conclusion. The rear-gunner's next would be his fiftieth operation, and so completed two full tours for him. He should then leave us, and go with honour to a screened appointment, but he decided otherwise, and applied to fly two extra sorties. He knew I valued his experience, and he didn't want to leave me with a novice gunner for the last two trips. I accepted his devotion without compunction, and without fuss.

We completed Charlie Two's numbered hours by taking her to Brunswick on 14 January, in an all-Lancaster attack. As we lounged beside the aircraft, waiting for Cassidy to join us with the latest forecasts, Protheroe offered round his cigarettes.

"Have one of my pontoon winnings, skipper."

"Well played, George."

"Hey, you know the Yanks went to Brunswick a couple of days ago? They got a hell of a pasting — lost sixty, I think it was."

"Well, it's a long way to go in daylight."

"Yeah, but I reckon they'll have stirred it up for us. I bet we don't half cop it."

"You are a cheerful little sod."

A staff car drew into the dispersal and stopped beside the aircraft. A raincoated civilian approached us, and introduced himself as an official photographer.

"I'd like to take a shot of your crew, with your aircraft in the background."

Walker combed his fingers through his tousled hair, and asked:

"Shall we get a copy of it, to send home?"

"You can all have copies, if you wish."

I unzipped my Irving jacket, and said:

"We always piddle on the tailwheel before we get on board. Would you like to take us doing that?"

The photographer smiled.

"That would make a nice group, certainly, but I don't think my editor would publish it."

Myring grinned wolfishly:

"You can come with us if you like, mate, and get some action pictures."

The photographer looked at me with interest, but I shook my head.

"No, he's only joking. I don't think we're allowed to take you."

The photograph was never published anyway, because the cigarettes that Myring and I were obviously smoking (others were being held out of sight) near large quantities of petrol and explosives, were too flagrant a breach of discipline to be officially advertised.

We crossed the foreign coast in daylight, and watched the guns on Texel take their toll of those off course. The weather was fine, the visibility unlimited, and Charlie Two growled resonantly in my ear as she passed from twilight into the familiar darkness. When Bremen lay to the north of us, I watched for yellow flares which PFF should drop to mark our route. Larry saw them first and raspingly reported their position, dead ahead on track. As Cassidy acknowledged, happily, this confirmation of his reckoning, there came a shock. A brilliant explosion blossomed out before me, so intense that all round turned black in contrast to its glaring colours. The nucleus seemed suspended, burning on our course, while subsidiary explosions spewed smoke-tailed fireballs out like rockets, and showers of green, white, red and golden light fell slowly from its midst.

Stiff with fright, and so blinded that I couldn't read the pallid figures on the instruments, I tried to reconcile the phenomenon with normality. I told myself: "This is a scarecrow flare, the sort we've been advised about. It doesn't frighten me." But still it fascinated me, as a car's headlights hold a frightened rabbit. It seemed to draw me, and to have the same effect on Charlie Two; for once she was sluggish in answering my touch, as though she wanted to engage the burning presence in our path. Even when I turned the nose away, the apparition seemed to stay ahead, as had the shadow aircraft that once came at me through a cloudscape. Flinching in my seat, I flew through the burning embers of that awful airborne pyre.

There were some places in Germany and the conquered lands where defences were so accurate and vicious that we took pains to keep out of their range when flying to and from the target. Such hot spots included the West Frisian Islands of Texel and Terschelling, Heligoland further north, and the subordinated towns of Amiens in Picardy, and Chartres. Over Germany itself, we had good reason to stay clear of Hanover, and so we extended our eastward leg to dodge those guns before we turned south-east for Brunswick. Nevertheless, we reached the target early, and I had to bring back the engines to dawdle so as not to drop the bombs before the zero hour of 7.15p.m.

The agitated hornet's nest didn't sting so sharply as Protheroe had adumbrated, but it was bad enough and

211

I was grateful when, for the last time in Charlie Two, I pushed the nose down to let the speed build up, and we moved south, out of the target area.

Five and a half hours after take-off, Charlie Two was on the landing-run at Wickenby, flirting with the runway as she liked to do, floating while I held her nose up to the last.

"Get down, you big, black bastard."

"Hey, take it back, Jack!"

"Sorry, sorry, get down you beaut. Have you got the power right off, Johnny?"

"I'll break the levers if I pull them any harder."

The main wheels whispered as they touched the concrete, and Charlie Two ran lightly down the centre-line. I squeezed the brake handle and turned her off the runway. I called the watch office.

"Charlie Two clear, over."

"Roger, Charlie Two."

"Okay, Johnny, flap up, do the checks."

"Right. Flaps up, booster pumps off, rad shutters open, pitot heater off."

Larry switched on the Aldis lamp, and shone it on the left-hand side of the taxiway to guide me to dispersal. While we waited for the crew bus, I piddled for the last time on Charlie Two's tailwheel, kicked the main wheels gently and wished her happy landings.

We had landed after the Brunswick raid at ten o'clock, unusually early, and were grateful for the full night's sleep, as we started six days' leave next day. Before departing in our various directions, we learned that the previous night had cost the Command nearly six per cent of the attacking force, including two from 626 Squadron. Another squadron aircraft, piloted by Flight Sergeant Jacques, had been extensively damaged during combat with a fighter. Awareness of the casualties enhanced the feeling of escape with which we packed our bags, donned best uniforms and greatcoats and took the transport into Lincoln.

At home I learned that a friend had been killed on an "Intruder" raid. For some time he had been flying Beaufighters and later Mosquitoes on these sorties, which involved flying into occupied territory or Germany to seek out homecoming enemy aircraft, and attack them in the circuit of their own airfields. We had our share of this treatment from the Luftwaffe too, and when we got the warning that "bandits" were about, on our return to Wickenby, we had to turn our navigation lights off and make do with restricted airfield lighting to guide us in the circuit.

One night, a Junkers 88 followed a returning Lancaster down the approach, meaning no doubt to strafe the bomber on the runway. The NCO in the runway caravan, however, took the German aircraft for one of ours and, knowing that only one was clear to land, shone the red Aldis lamp in the enemy pilot's face. The latter appeared to be so taken aback by this that he overshot, and was seen no more. Perhaps he was short of fuel or out of ammunition, but anyway the caravan ACP got the credit for seeing him off.

I had no strong views about the pilots of the night-fighters who opposed us in the campaign over

Germany, and certainly no antipathy, until the night I saw a bomber crew bale out over the western suburbs of Berlin, and the pilot of an Mel09 fired burst after burst of gunfire at the figures swinging helplessly below their parachutes. First I felt sickened at the scene, silhouetted against the fires and smoke below, then I grew hot with anger at the bloody, vengeful act. I mentioned the incident later in the flight office, and said that now I took a harsher view of German pilots.

"I'm finished with all that balls about the Jerry pilots being just like us. I couldn't have shot those parachutes up."

The Gunnery Leader shrugged, and commented:

"He may have been a Berliner himself, and he might have lost a wife, or his favourite popsy, in a raid last week. You never know."

"Okay, and so have some of our chaps lost relatives in the blitz, but it hasn't turned them into murderous bastards, like that fellow."

"How do you know it hasn't? It's a murderous bloody war, old mate."

CHAPTER
NINE

Big City Finish

As usual, I passed the leisure time peacefully, relishing my mother's cooking and looking up the lads and lasses of the village. On Wednesday, I went with mother and sister to the West End to see Terence Rattigan's new play *While the Sun Shines*, enjoying the comedy, the piquancy of Jane Baxter, and the urbane style of Ronald Squire.

Since childhood, the twin boys John and Paul had been my friends. They joined the RAF a few months after I did, and followed me to the USA for pilot training. There they were commissioned and, as I had feared would have been my lot if I hadn't disqualified myself, remained in America as instructors. Now they were home, enjoying disembarkation leave and hoping for posting to a bomber squadron. I joined them in the Queen's Head, in Pinner's steeply sloping High Street, and over the drinks we swopped stories of our doings since last we met; of theirs at the flying school in Texas with the evocative name of Waco; of mine with the crew and the Lancasters at Wickenby. It was good to see them sitting there, laughing together by the fireside in the cosy, oak-beamed bar-room. John was a happy-go-lucky, mischief-loving fellow, a contrast to his steady brother of classic features and courteous manners. Their sum of qualities, too great for any one person but a paragon, exemplified for me the best in man.

It was John who asked if he could spend the last few days of his leave with me at Wickenby, and I was glad to have his company on the railway journey back to Lincoln on Sunday 23 January. We stayed that night at the Saracen's Head, and Mr Kirk's taxi took us sedately to the airfield in the morning. I asked Bill Spiller, the Flight Commander, if I might take John flying in the Lancaster. ME589 needed to have her bomb-sight levelled and John, bubbling with pleasure and excitement, joined the crew as second pilot for the detail. When Larry had completed the business with the bomb-sight to his grudging satisfaction, we spent a happy quarter of an hour putting the aircraft through her paces.

That night we stayed again in Lincoln, accompanied by the fun-loving George Gerrard, McLaughlin's Canadian gunner, and plagued the stiff head waiter about the rabbit camouflaged as chicken when we dined at the Saracen's Head. John retained his room there, while Gerrard and I put up at the less pretentious Great Northern Hotel. John wanted to fly with me on an operation, but I didn't like the idea of facing Paul if I got his brother shot up, and I wasn't too disappointed (although John was) when Spiller turned the idea down. However, I obtained permission for John to stay on camp for the remainder of his leave, and he moved into a vacant bed in my hut.

The air test of the previous day was to be the only flight John ever had in a Lancaster, for he and Paul were posted to a squadron in Yorkshire where they flew and died in Halifaxes. John was on a minelaying sortie to the Kiel canal. His body was found by Danish villagers and given good burial beside the sea. A month later, while the main force struck a terrible blow at Dresden, Paul's choice was to follow his brother's route to Kiel. His sacrifice is marked in stone at Runnymede, where stand memorials to those of no known grave.

On Thursday, 27 January, we were briefed for Berlin again, in pursuance of the Commander-in-Chief's expressed intention to destroy the German capital. The campaign, which had begun in late November, now was at its height. The enemy knew that the current odds were on the Big City being our target, and his defensive tactics had improved. He had a couple of new radar devices, one airborne and the other on the ground, which weren't so easily upset by "window" as their predecessors were. He had developed the use of decoy targets and of fighter flares, while the number and calibre of his flak guns had increased. We too had made advances. There was much more use of electronic jamming, better navigation aids, spoof attacks to draw the fighters off, and feints to keep the enemy controllers guessing as to which the target city was.

That Howe Two which we took to Bochum in September had gone from Wickenby, and had served with several other squadrons since. The new Howe Two was JB559, originally a 12 Squadron aircraft, now with 626, and a thoroughly poor specimen of her type. She was sluggish in response to the controls, and lacked the Lancaster's characteristic stability in night. She wouldn't stay on course, constantly dropped one wing or the other, and needed frequent adjustment of the elevator trim to maintain an even height. She brought home to me the loss of Charlie Two, whose steadiness and ease of manoeuvre I had so long accepted as a right.

We crossed the enemy coast north of Bremerhaven, heading as though to strike at Magdeburg, then turned east to cross the Elbe near Wittenburg, continuing eastward until Berlin lay on the starboard beam. We bombed the target on a course of 150°, and turned south-west to pass by Leipzig on our right. Forty miles or so further on we came to Zeitze, where a railway met the river, and turned westward for one long leg to reach the coast of France, directly into a headwind of 100mph. The coastline lay 450 miles away, and the prospect of the journey chilled me. It typified the most unpleasant features of bomber operations; utter physical boredom, and the nagging fear of unknown hazards lying in wait. I called the navigator.

"Jim, is there any way we can duck this headwind? Would we make a better ground speed if I went down lower?"

"Aw, no, not really, Jack. The way our true airspeed would drop off would just about match the fall in wind speed."

"I was afraid of that."

"The wind may veer a bit as we get further west, but not enough to make much difference to the ground speed."

"Okay, we press on at this height."

The clouds swept past us swiftly, but the ground beneath them scarcely seemed to move. The river Saale glinted briefly, and the darkened towns of Weimar, Erfurt and Gotha crawled by, identifiable only by their names upon the map. It had taken Howe Two nearly half an hour to cover fifty miles. The journey taxed us all, and none more so than Myring, who regularly expressed his feelings as we lurched unsteadily along.

"Eh, skip, it's a bloody long stooge though, ain't it?"

"Yes, Larry."

"Cripes, but I'm bloody uncomfortable down here."

"Yes, Larry."

I tried the automatic pilot; Howe Two raised her nose sharply, and began to make a slow roll to the right. I took "George" out and, having centralised the trimmers, tried again. Howe Two attempted a flick roll to the left. Cassidy commented:

"You will let me know if you're making any course alterations, won't you?"

"No change, Jimmy. Just playing with 'George', but he's not in the mood."

"You're still on two-six-five?"

"Two-six-five it is."

I accepted the obvious incompatibility of Howe Two and "George", and settled down to fly the brute myself.

"Eh, skip, have you got the heater turned off?"

"No, Larry, it's on full. The wireless-op's suffocating."

"He wants to come down here with me, then. That'd cool 'im off."

Ninety minutes later we passed between Bonn and Koblenz, and still the map of Europe seemed to spread unceasingly ahead. I brooded on the possibility of using more power from the engines, and sounded out the engineer.

"Let's have a few more revs, Johnny."

"What about the fuel consumption?"

"What about it?"

"Well, d'you want enough left for a diversion when we get back?"

I thought at this speed we're never going to get back. I said:

"There won't be any fog, with this wind blowing all over Europe."

"Hm. What do you want, then?"

"Pour the coal on. Put 'em up a hundred revs."

"Okay. Up a hundred."

The Belgian towns of Namur and Charleroi passed below while Howe Two, after long deliberation, grudgingly responded to our urging and showed an added five mph on the ASI. My hands were cold; I beat them on my knees to stimulate the circulation. The woollen gloves I wore were inadequate protection for so chill a temperature. I had a pair of silken inner gloves, but I disliked the feel of them next to my skin, and didn't wear them; the big leather gauntlets were too clumsy for handling the knobs and switches in the cockpit. We wallowed across the plains of Artois.

"Cripes, but I'm cheesed with this trip. How much further is it to the coast?"

"Not far now, Larry. You should see it in about ten minutes."

"I don't know why, but I can't seem to get any bloody heat through."

At last the English Channel stretched before us, and we turned to aim at Dungeness. Once again, we were first home to Wickenby, where we learned that three of ours were among the thirty missing. One was flown by Squadron Leader Goule, most stentorian of voices at a sing-song, who was nearing the end of his second tour. Another was that of Colin Grannum, who came down in Belgium, fought with the Maquis and, eventually, returned to England. The third was Noel Belford, shot down far away among the Taurus mountains, where this time neither the Royal Navy, nor anyone else, could help.

We crept into the huts at three o'clock, by which time I longed for the embrace of sheets and blankets, and to lay my face against the softness of the pillow. I fumbled with my clothing in the darkness, but John awoke, and propped himself up on his elbow.

"How did it go?"

"All right, John. Strong headwind all the way home, though. Took us ages. Did you get supper?"

"Yes, man, after I'd watched the take-off. One didn't get away, and a couple came back early. Were the rest okay?"

"Three were still missing when we left interrogation, but we were first back. Beat the next one by six minutes."

John scratched his fair head, and grinned.

"Bet you feel good now, don't you, with only one to go?"

"Yeah, John, one to go. It might take us a while to get it in; they usually try to give you an easy trip to finish on, you know, Wraps France or Italy, so we might have to wait around a bit."

"Anything I can get you? D'you want a cigarette?"

"No, thanks. Go back to sleep, John."

"Good-night, man, see you in the morning."

"Good-night, John. Wake me at the crack of noon."

Myring bustled in at half past ten next morning, as I was idly wondering whether or not to pass another hour in bed. His eyes were red-rimmed, and his tie was askew.

"We're on again tonight, Jack. Same petrol load, same bloody bomb load. Looks like the Big City again. Wouldn't it root you?"

I sat up and stared at him.

"Are you sure?"

"Sure I'm sure. Main briefing four o'clock."

I struggled out of the comforting clutches of the bed.

"I'll see the Flight Commander. He promised us an easy one to finish on."

"Good on you, skip."

The Flight Commander looked up anxiously when I marched into his office, and raised a placatory hand.

"I know what you're going to say, Jack, but I'm thinking of your own best interests, honestly."

"Oh, yeah. Best interests be blowed. Berlin two nights running isn't my best interests anytime, and certainly not for our last two trips. Don't you think we've been there often enough?"

"I know that, Jack, but . . ."

"Last night made the eighth Big City op in my log-book."

"Will you listen a moment? I've seen chaps hanging around waiting for their last op. getting more and more jittery . . ."

"I'm bloody jittery now."

"No, you're not, you haven't had time to be. It's a seven o'clock take-off, you'll be home by three, and you're finished before you've had a chance to worry about it."

"Oh, balls!"

"Balls or not, it's the best way, Jack."

"All right, all right, you're the boss. But if we get the chop on this one, I'm coming back to haunt you, Bill, and you'll never sleep sound again."

"Good luck, chum."

The take-off was postponed for an hour, and we waited at dispersal. Sometimes such delays augured cancellation of the mission, and the coward deep inside me whispered hopes to that effect. It was hardly worth our while to clamber from the aircraft, but we did, and, while Bretell remained to clean once more his turret's perspex, the rest of us gathered in the ground crew's hut. Protheroe enviously eyed four airmen who were playing cards on an upturned packing case; Cassidy entered some refinements in his navigation log; Myring produced a paper-backed thriller and squatted on the floor, using his weight to command a position near the stove. Walker untied the tapes of his Mae West, and passed me a cigarette.

"What d'you reckon, Jack? Scrub?"

"Blowed if I know, Johnny. The weather looked all right at briefing; I can't see why we shouldn't go."

Protheroe grinned.

"Goodoh! Off on leave tomorrow, and no more ops!"

"It's a nice thought, isn't it?"

"Yeah, I'm looking forward to saying 'up yours' to old man chop."

He illustrated his remark with an appropriate two-fingered gesture. Myring frowned, and wagged his head.

"Don't count yer chickens yet, young George. It's still a bloody long way to Berlin and back."

Walker felt obliged to speak up for the aircraft.

"Not with these new props and engines. We'll be in and out like a Mossie."

"Aw, gimme ole Charlie Two any day. This bloody thing's built in Canada, isn't it? What do they know about building Lancasters?"

"No, Larry, listen. You've got it all wrong . . ."

Fairbairn broke in, reflectively:

"Talking about Charlie Two, I wonder where our old tail-end Charlie is tonight?"

"Lanham? He'll be fast asleep in bed while we're at twenty thousand feet, if he's got any sense."

"How does it feel, Jack, not to have him riding hard on you any more? You can go on the piss any time you want to, now."

"No, I can't. Larry drinks it all before I get there."

Fairbairn looked at me with his slow smile.

"I'll never forget how you and Charlie taught me to smoke, so you could cadge cigs off me, when you were short."

Cassidy looked up from his figures.

"That Lanham! I hope he finds his coral island, and the twenty-foot fishing boat he used to go on about."

A ground-crew sergeant pushed his way into the hut, and gave a brief salute.

"Message from control: take-off's postponed another four hours. First kite's due off at midnight. The crew bus is coming out to pick you up."

I felt another tingle of resentment. What a horrid op to finish on — two postponements and a midnight take-off! Cassidy got to his feet beside me, stowing away his paper work.

"What are you going to do? Try and get your head down for a few hours?"

"Honestly, Jim, I don't think I'd sleep. What's on at the cinema?"

"*Casablanca.*"

"Seen it."

"I haven't. Is it worth seeing?"

"Yes, it's good. Matter of fact, I'm not sure I wouldn't rather sit through it again than hang around the mess for three hours."

We fumbled our way to seats in the already darkened cinema, and let ourselves become engrossed in Ingrid Bergman's candid eyes and tremulous mouth, in Humphrey Bogart's rasping lisp, and in the little coloured pianist as he aptly sang "As Time Goes By". Those performers must have had some magic, to make time go by for us with some degree of pleasure and of calm. Only the distant rumble of a Merlin, being test-run on the airfield, occasionally pierced the sound-track and caused my heart to miss a beat.

At seven minutes after midnight Fox Two's Packard-built Merlins were in steady song, and the Hamilton propellers, with their blades like canoe paddles, had turned to shadow circles in the darkness. At 0008hrs she rolled out of her dispersal and round the winding taxi-way to the take-off marshalling point. I twitched the brake lever on and off, on and off, and brought her to a halt.

"Okay, Johnny, checks. Throttles." "Set on a thousand."

"Trims, elevator two notches nose down." "Elevator and aileron trims neutral."

"Supercharger?"

"M gear."

"Pitch?"

"Fully fine and locked." "Pitot-heater on. Fuel?" "Contents checked, master cocks on, cross-feed off, boosters on."

"Flaps?"

"One third down, and reading." "Gills?"

"Air intake cold, rad shutters auto."

"George — clutch in, cock out. Gyro — compass set."

I saw the green light of the caravan from the corner of my eye, nursing my night vision by not looking directly at the lamp, and released the brakes. At eighteen minutes after midnight, Fox Two shot into the air as though she were the first jet-engined bomber. The engine gauges showed eighteen pounds of boost when I pushed the throttles through the takeoff gate, that was fifty per cent more power than Charlie Two developed at her best. As she climbed easily over Wickenby, vibrant and responsive in my hands, I acknowledged that my wishes for a less formidable target were craven and unmanly. Berlin was the proper target for our final mission. And Bill was right: it was best to get it over with minimum delay.

"Nav to pilot. It's 0044 on my watch now; will you set course 094 degrees for Mablethorpe in one minute?"

"094 compass, Jim. Hey, this thing is climbing at about four hundred feet a minute. She's quite an aeroplane."

"Goodoh, Jack. Let me know when you're on course."

Quarter of an hour later, we crossed the Lincolnshire coast at 17,000 feet and set course for Denmark, 360 miles away, and halfway to the target. Over the North Sea, Fox Two reached her operating altitude of 20,000 feet, and Walker pulled the pitch levers back to keep the ASI showing 150mph. With the westerly wind and thinner air to help, we were passing over the water at 250mph. At 0212hrs we were off the Danish coast, and altered course due east. Seven minutes later, Myring growled on the intercom.

"Nav from bomb-aimer. Red marker flares ahead on track."

"Thanks, Larry. That's where they should be. Let me know when we're overhead."

Fairbairn picked up a broadcast on the wind velocity, which had been computed and passed back for us by a leading PFF navigator. It gave a wind from 310° at 87mph, and Cassidy found one from his airplot from the same direction at 84mph. He was satisfied with this, and at 0239hrs his dead reckoning put us at our turning point for the long leg to Berlin.

"Nav to pilot. Turn on to 162°. ETA on target is 0325."

"162 it is, Jim."

Half an hour later, Myring reported the next set of route-markers going down to port of our track. I turned Fox Two to overfly them.

"Nav to pilot. When you're over the markers, turn on to a new course for the target of 150°. The wind's veering a bit and strengthening."

"150°, roger."

"And, Jack, can you bring the airspeed back by five? We're making a ground speed of 280, and it's going to make us early."

"Wilco."

I saw the first target-indicators go down at 0310hrs, and steered ten degrees to port to bring us over them. I let Fox Two climb a couple of hundred feet to clear somebody's slipstream which was rocking her unpleasantly. At 0318hrs a vast explosion shook the city, its blast waves spreading like the concentric ripples radiated by a stone thrown into a still pool. Two minutes later Myring pressed the release button, and our last bomb load fell upon Berlin.

I turned on to 119° for our route out of the target, and let the speed build up to 200mph on the ASI. The wind was now from 315° at 95mph, which gave us an extraordinary ground speed of 368mph. I should have held that course for three minutes, but now I saw that it was lit on either side by slowly falling fighter flares. It looked as though peace-time Oxford Street had been suspended in the sky above Berlin.

"Pilot to nav. I don't like this course, Jim. It's leading straight to trouble. I'm going to cut the corner."

"Okay, Jack. Make it 027° if you can, then we'll be about right at the next turning point."

I headed Fox Two out of the lighted thoroughfare, and sought a darker piece of sky. This was one time when I felt it safer to be out of the stream. At 0326hrs Cassidy estimated that we had reached the turning point, and we altered course north-west, straight into the wind which the latest broadcast told us, blew from

320 degrees at 95mph. Fox Two's ground speed fell to 144mph as she met the moving air. Now there were no route markers to guide us, and we were far outside the range at which the G-box might give help. Cassidy resorted to his last remaining aid.

"Nav to pilot. Can you see the stars?"

"Yes, Jim, loud and clear."

"Goodoh. I'll try a couple of shots."

He stood for several minutes in the astrodome, letting his eyes become accustomed to the darkness. When he was ready to use the sextant, I settled myself more firmly in the seat and concentrated on making Fox Two a level platform while he took the shots. The blue star Vega gave him a good line, but the shot of Spica, brightest of the stars in Virgo, didn't match it, and he wasn't much the wiser for his efforts. At quarter past four, Rostock should have been on the starboard beam, but we saw no sign of it, and Myring couldn't see the line of Lübeck Bay through the drifts of stratus cloud below. At 0440hrs came the first sign since we left the target that anyone in Germany was awake.

"Pilot to nav. Bags of heavy flak ahead. Where would that be?"

"Should be Kiel, Jack. I think we're a bit port of track."

"Okay, I'll go north of it. Turning on to 330°."

"Will you let me know when it's on the port beam, then?"

"Wilco."

After a few minutes I had to alter course again to avoid the gunfire of a flak ship lying in Kiel Bay, then, at three minutes past five, we turned on Cassidy's ETA to fly along the fifty-fifth parallel across the Danish mainland. At 0519hrs I gave the guns of Sylt a wide berth to our south, and gently lowered Fox Two's nose to bring up 200mph on the ASI. Soon Europe was behind us, and only 360 miles of cold North Sea lay between us and the coast of England. Protheroe's Welsh intonation sang on the intercom:

"So long, chop-land. And if I never see you again, it'll be too soon."

"Pilot to crew. Well played, you people. Specially you, Len, thanks for staying with us."

Bretell replied primly from the rear turret.

"Thank you, skipper. It's been a pleasure."

"Okay, now let's see how fast this super-Lanc can get us back to base."

Cassidy picked up his first G signals at six o'clock, still 250 miles away from England, and from then on navigated down the G-chart's lattice lines. Walker had the rpm right back for minimum fuel consumption, but Fox Two settled to a steady 210mph indicated, and it was all I could do to persuade her to lose height. Our flight-plan time for Mablethorpe was 0737, but we saw the friendly searchlight at 0658, right ahead on track. We were over Wickenby at 0717, and I made a careful circuit.

"Darky from Fox Two — funnels."

"Fox Two, you are clear to land. Congratulations on completing your tour over."

"Thank you, Darky — out."

We landed thirty minutes before the next aircraft to come home. That was Reg Wellham, who had bombed the target two minutes ahead of us. Even so, Fox Two had 460 gallons of fuel left in her tanks, and Walker was delighted.

"Well, Larry, what d'you think of her now, eh?"

"Aw, she's okay, I suppose. You can't really tell from one trip, though, can you? I mean, we did a lot in old Charlie Two."

I joined them in the crew bus.

"You mean you want to do some more in Fox Two, Larry? Shall I sign us on for another tour?"

"No bloody fear, skip. Well, give a man a chance to have a rest."

By half past seven, Cassidy, Myring and I were in the officers' mess. A crate of beer had been put out for us by courtesy of my flight commander. Jim was still teetotal, and beer was not the beverage I relished at that hour, but Larry did his best to make up for our shortcomings. I took a token gulp.

"Cheers, Bill. Okay, so you were right. You can sleep easy, you old bastard."

"Cheers, Jack. I'm glad of that. The Old Man's in the dining room, and he's got the AOC with him. They want you to join them for breakfast."

"Oh, Christ, no!"

"Oh, Christ, yes. Honestly, the AOC's come up from Group especially."

"I reckon they only put these late ops on so that they can see us in without staying up late."

"Take your beer in with you — they won't mind. Go on, you miserable sod!"

John and I caught the London train from Lincoln in the early afternoon. He had a first class ticket, and mine was third, but I stretched out on a seat in his compartment and fell asleep. I'd had seven hours' sleep in the last fifty odd, and it took a loud altercation between John and the ticket-collector to waken me. I heard a snatch of it before going to sleep again.

"I don't care if he bombed Berlin every night for a week. I've got my job to do as well, and that's all there is about it . . ."

I got home at seven-thirty in the evening, twelve hours after our last landing at Wickenby. An unprecedented fortnight's leave stretched like an eternity of ease ahead of me. For once, I went to church on Sunday, accompanying my mother out of deference to her wish to express gratitude for the crew's survival. I played billiards with my father, and went to the cinema with my sister. We spent a few days in Devon, staying with an aunt and uncle in the salubrity of Sidmouth. I hadn't my uncle's capacity for whisky, and I was noisier and unsteadier than he as we walked homeward from the nearby hotel bar.

Sometimes I thought about the others: Lanham was kicking his heels in Scotland, waiting for a ship to take him home. Cassidy was staying with relatives in Ireland; Protheroe was in Pembrokeshire, Walker in the Wirral, Fairbairn in Northumberland, Myring only he knew where. As the lazy leave days dwindled, I began to think about the future. We would be "screened" from operations for a while, and posted to training units as instructors. We were no longer a crew, but individual airmen, each with a separate task and destiny, no more a part of one another's fate.

Back at Wickenby, I looked at the notice board for news of our postings, and found it briefly stated:

P/O J. A. L. Currie 155488 Pilot	1656 Con Unit
P/O H. E. Myring Aus 400816 A/B	27 OTU
F/O J. Cassidy Aus 414901 Nav	1662 Con Unit
1830250 Sgt Protheroe A/G	82 OTU
1078762 Sgt Fairbairn WO/Air	83 OTU
1624293 Sgt Walker F/Eng	1662 Con Unit

Woody was the Chief Instructor at 1662 Conversion Unit, near Gainsborough, and a couple of telephone calls switched my posting to that airfield. At least I would have Cassidy as a mess-mate, and Walker could still fly with me as engineer. We spent an evening drinking with the ground crew who had tended Charlie Two so well, and then prepared for our departure.

Cycling round the Station with a clearance chit, I remembered our first sight of Wickenby, of the drab hangars and the watertower standing in the pallid sunshine, and of the black Lancasters crouching on the airfield. As I passed the operations block, I recalled the first time we filed in for briefing, and the stomach-tensing sense of purpose in that brightly lit, smoke-filled room. I saw the ranks of bicycles, propped outside the double doors, and remembered the way that Lanham used to free-wheel up to join us, standing on the near-side pedal, then stepping nonchalantly off, leaving the cycle to run on and find its own parking place, with a crash, among the rest.

I loitered among the crew as they were packing, toying with their belongings, making desultory wisecracks and getting in their way. I wanted to let them know how much I hated parting from them, without committing the solecism of actually saying so.

We boarded the transport, laden with our baggage. Out on the airfield a Merlin engine coughed twice, then burst into full-throated song. Our driver shut the door, and we settled on the bench seats.

"They'll never finish the war without us, skip. I can see the headlines in *Die Berliner Zeitung*: 'Currie's crew screened new hope for doomed city'."

"We'll come back on a second tour soon, and finish 'em off."

"Yeah, well, let's have a tour on wine, women and song first."

"A tour on circuit-bashing with sprog crews, you mean."

"I don't fancy flying with sprogs."

The WAAF driver turned the truck carefully into the Wragby road, which glistened damply under the pale, grey sky. I looked at the crew, unfamiliar in their best blue, with respirator cases hanging from their shoulders.

"Christ, Johnny, don't you ever clean your boots?"

"I haven't got a nice, little batwoman to bull my stuff, you know. Actually, I haven't worn them for so long they seem to have gone a bit dull."

"Dull? There's a cobweb on one of them."

"Bollocks."

Seen through the back window of the truck as we ran down the hill in Lincoln, the cathedral loomed above us, beautiful and strong. It looked so balanced, so symmetrical and so permanent that our existence seemed the more precarious, our presence utterly transitory. Myring glanced at his wrist-watch.

"Hey, I reckon we've got time for one at the Northern before my train — what do you say?"

Fairbairn put the question warily:

"Have you got any money?"

"I've got enough to buy you sods one last drink, anyway."

"It'll be the first you've bought for flipping weeks."

"All right, all right. This is sort of a special occasion, isn't it? Do you want it, or don't you?"

I pulled my gaze away from the cathedral.

"Okay, Larry. Let's have one for the road."

"Good on yer, skip. Cripes, I'm dry."

Cassidy tugged his peaked cap straighter on his head.

"I don't know. All you beggars think about is grog."

"Be in it, Jim. You can have a grapefruit."

"What makes you think I want to be seen in a pub with you blokes?"

They bickered on as the driver sorted out the gears at the bottom of the hill. The cathedral filled less of the window now, but still it dwarfed the city. I thought: this is where I turn the last page of this chapter, and say farewell to this small company. I'll leave my thoughts with the cathedral, and let them stay in that security, while we take our different roads away from here, away from Wickenby and the bombers.

Also available in ISIS Large Print:

A Somerset Airman

Eric Gardner

At the age of 19, Eric Gardner joined the RAF. His witty observations of day-to-day life as an airman in wartime Britain and Canada give a fascinating insight into the life experienced by many ordinary men and women, from all backgrounds, who were brought together by World War Two.

Like many of his generation, Eric did not receive a higher education and was unable to fulfil his obvious potential. In later life, he often commented that the RAF had been his university.

Eric thought his wartime experiences would be of little interest to anyone else because he did not see any active service. His family thankfully did not agree and encouraged him to commit his memories to paper. He finished the manuscript just days before his sudden death at the age of 82 and so, sadly, Eric never saw it in print.

ISBN 0-7531-9352-3 (hb)
ISBN 0-7531-9353-1 (pb)

They Also Serve

Dorothy Baden-Powell

At the Scandinavian Section of the SOE, Dorothy Baden-Powell was engaged in sending saboteurs into occupied Norway and debriefing them on their return to London. After spending a year and a half with the SOE, she was given an assignment in the WRNS to try to break a ring of enemy spies. They were based on HMS *Raleigh*, a naval training camp at Plymouth and were sending information to Germany about the movements of British warships from nearly every port in the United Kingdom.

She endured the privations of life on the lower deck, the unwelcome scrutiny of a particularly unpleasant WRNS Superintendent, and a trumped-up charge and subsequent court-martial.

Finally, she uncovered an enemy agent trying to be taken on as a sailor, and by a combination of bravery, sheer determination and luck, succeeded in having him captured. With her assignment successfully completed she gladly returned to her job with the SOE.

ISBN 0-7531-9336-1 (hb)
ISBN 0-7531-9337-X (pb)